CW00590469

JOSIAH MASON 1795 - 1881
Birmingham's Benevolent Benefactor

To Pete

Best wishes

Brian Jones

First published in February 1995 by
Brewin Books, Studley, Warwickshire, B80 7LG
Reprinted January 1999.

© Brian Jones

ISBN 1 85858 042 0

All rights reserved.

To members of the
Erdington Historical Society

By the same author:
Brian Jones and Margaret Rawcliffe,
Llanddulas Heritage of a Village,
Gee & Son, 1985

Front cover illustration:
Mason's Science College

Made and printed in Great Britain by
Supaprint (Redditch) Ltd.

Josiah Mason 1795 - 1881
Birmingham's Benevolent Benefactor

List of Illustrations

Frontispiece: Sir Josiah Mason
1. Entry of Baptism of Josiah Mason.   2
2. Entry of marriage Josiah Mason and Annie Griffiths.   3
3. Birthplace of Josiah Mason at Mill Street Kidderminster.   6
4. Existing house on site of Josiah Mason's birthplace 1992.   7
5. Plaque on house - birthplace site, Josiah Mason.   7
6. Sketch of Mason as a boy selling bread from door to door.   8
7. Sketch of Mason as a boy with donkey "Admiral Rodney".   9
8. Mason's first workplace in Birmingham the Aston Flint Glass   11
    Works of B&W Gibbins.
9. The house in Bagot Street, Birmingham where Mason and his   11
    wife Annie lived.
10. Wesleyan Chapel, Mill Street, Kidderminster.   14
11. Belmont Row Wesleyan Chapel, Birmingham.   15
12. Annie, Mason's wife.   16
13. Josiah Mason surrounded by signs of his achievements.   22
14. Perry & Co. pen-nibs on display at the Birmingham Museum   28
    of Science and Industry.
15. Lancaster Street, Birmingham Mason's Pen Works.   29
16. Sketches of pen making process.   30-32
17. Mason pen-nib samples roll.   35
18. Sir Josiah Mason pens price list.   36
19. Plan of Lancaster Street Pen Works.   37
20. Perry & Company Limited notice to customers.   41
21. Elkington, Mason & Co., Electroplating Works, Newhall Street.   46
22. G.R. Elkington.   47
23. Part of the electroplating process.   48
24. Commemoration Shield designed for Great Exhibition 1851.   49
25. Elkington, Mason & Co., showrooms Birmingham.   50
26. (a) Remains of Mason & Elkington's Copperworks Pembrey, S.Wales.   53
    (b) Copperworks School built 1855.   54
27. First almshouses and orphanage built by Mason 1858.   57
28. Second and main orphanage built by Mason, Bell Lane, Erdington,   61
    1868
29. Orphanage Erdington - principal staircase.   62
30. Map of Erdington and surrounding area 1881.   66
31. Sir Josiah Mason's Orphanage rules for visitors.   67
32. Demolition of the orphanage.   70
33. Sir Josiah Mason's Orphanage.   73
34. Sir Josiah Mason.   75
35. Dormitory - Mason's Orphanage Erdington.   77
36. Kitchen - Mason's Orphanage Erdington.   78
37. Dining Hall - Mason's Orphanage Erdington.   80
38. Sir Josiah Mason.   82

39.	Mason Science College ground floor plan.	90
40.	Mason Science College Birmingham.	91
41.	Mason Science College opening ceremony 1 October, 1880.	93
42.	Mason University College Council Room 1897.	94
43.	Mason University College Physics Laboratory 1897.	94
44.	Statue of Mermaid from Mason College.	95
45.	Plaque marking site of Mason College.	97
46.	Company details Birmingham, Erdington & Sutton Coldfield railway.	99
47.	Birmingham Banking Company details.	101
48.	Homeopathic Hospital, Easy Row, Birmingham.	102
49.	Dr. J. Gibbs Blake.	104
50.	J. Thackray Bunce.	104
51.	L.H. Elkington, T.P. Heslop, G.J. Johnson and M. Pollack.	105
52.	Woodbrooke, Northfield, Birmingham.	108
53.	Berwood, Chester Road, Erdington.	108
54.	Norwood House, Erdington, Birmingham.	109
55.	Letter from Prime Minister Gladstone offering Knighthood 1872.	111
56.	Portrait of Sir Josiah Mason by H.T. Munns 1872.	112
57.	Handwritten letter by Mason to H. Penn 1880.	114
58.	Statue of Mason Chester Road, Erdington.	115
59.	Annie Mason, Sir Josiah's wife.	119
60.	Mausoleum in the orphanage grounds Erdington.	120
61.	Childrens' burial place in orphanage grounds.	125
62.	Plaque at Perry Barr Crematorium.	126

Illustration Acknowledgements

1.	Hereford and Worcester County Council, Kidderminster Library:	1, 3, 10
2.	Frances Walsh:	7
3.	Birmingham City Council, Reference Library:	2, 11, 12, 23, 27-29, 31, 32, 34-38, 40, 41, 47, 51, 53-55, 57, 59-61
4.	Birmingham Mail:	9
5.	Philip Poole, London:	13, 15, 16, 17
6.	Birmingham City Council, Museum of Science and Industry:	15, 21
7.	Manchester City Council, Libraries Department, Renold Archive:	18, 19, 20
8.	Birmingham City Council, Museums and Art Gallery:	24
9.	R.J. Hugh Lewis and David R. Nicholson, Burry Port, Dyfed:	26a
10.	David R Nicholson and Stuart I. Parker, Burry Port, Dyfed:	26b
11.	University of Birmingham, Library:	39, 42, 43, 44, 56
12.	Society of Friends, Woodbrooke College, Birmingham:	52

Contents

List of Illustrations iv
Illustration Acknowledgements v
Acknowledgements vii
Chapter 1   Introduction 1
Chapter 2   Humble Origins and Self Help 6
Chapter 3   Religious Views and Influences 14
Chapter 4   Milestones on the Road to Success 21
Chapter 5   Penmaking 27
Chapter 6   Enterprise in Partnership 45
Chapter 7   Orphanage 56
Chapter 8   Orphan's Reminiscences 71
Chapter 9   Science College 85
Chapter 10   Public Image and Power 98
Chapter 11   Conclusions 117

Appendices
1. Family Tree 127
2. Notes of Will 128
3. Mason's friends and associates by occupation, politics, religion 133
   and membership of Birmingham organisations.
Bibliography 135
Index 142

Acknowledgements

The origins of this book stem from an interest in local history developed over many years, but the more immediate inspiration was the friendly support and enthusiasm of members of the Erdington Historical Society. Particular mention must be made of the late Geoff Hitchman, who gave unselfishly of his knowledge and records, never failing to find some reference to Mason in the work he was undertaking, and Kay Van Kesteren who always managed to answer my Erdington queries.

I have also called on the knowledge and resources of the Birmingham City Council, Reference Library, particularly Patrick Baird, and staff employed in the History and Geography, and Archives Departments, also Dr. J.H. Andrews of the Museum of Science and Industry, Martin Ellis of the Museum and Art Gallery, also Christine Penney of the University of Birmingham Library, Christina Lawson, Society of Friends, Woodbrooke College, Judith Baldry of Manchester City Library, Local Studies Department, Miss Hart of Kidderminster Library, staff of the Dyfed County Council, Record Office, The Victoria and Albert Museum, Archive of Art and Design, The British Library, Newspaper Library, and Companies House.

Thanks are also extended to my brother Ken, who carried out some of the research, my sister Yvonne, the indexing, Philip Poole who gave unstinting of his vast knowledge of the pen trade, and gave many pointers for further research, Ted Bonner who kindly took photographs, Ralph Jones who applied his computer skills to great advantage, Simon Williams who gave me much help, and John Findlay for detailed information.

Special thanks are due to my Tutor Bob Cromarty at Wolverhampton University, Mr. T.S. Wallace, Director of the Sir Josiah Mason Trust, to my wife Edna who made it possible for me to spend time producing this book, and to Catherine Beasley, who has spent hours formatting, indexing and reproducing it in a presentable form.

Frontispiece

Chapter 1
Introduction

Although there is little physical evidence of Mason's achievements to be seen in present day Birmingham, his impact upon the life of the Nineteenth Century town was considerable. His industrial ingenuity and charitable generosity cannot be underestimated. Mason himself was something of an enigma, living through a period of great social, political and economic upheaval, and yet not becoming directly involved in politics.

Bunce's biography of Mason written in 1882, a year after Mason's death, was based on Bunce's recollections and conversation with him. For Bunce - the first historian of the Corporation of Birmingham - to have interested himself in such a work was some indication of Mason's standing in the community. Published for private circulation, it was followed in 1890 by an amended and enlarged edition published by Chambers, containing additional chapters on the pen-making, and electroplating industries. Written in the somewhat eulogistic prose of the Victorian era, they present a sympathetic and detailed account of his life and work. However, neither edition address the issues surrounding his personality, motivation, authority and influence as an entrepreneur and philanthropist.

Other biographical material including the contributions of Taylor, Wedley, and Beale, use Bunce as their main source of reference, and all were written to meet the demands of a contemporary market. Beale's account is interesting, in that it differs from the others in its scathing references to Mason as selfish and uncharitable, but adds nothing further to our understanding of his personality. This literature presents him as retiring, self-effacing, taking no part in public life, living a somewhat isolated and frugal existence.

Mason was born at Kidderminster, Worcestershire on 23 February 1795,(1) and was baptised at the Parish Church, St. Mary and All Saints on the 27 March of the same year. He was the third child of Josiah Mason of Kidderminster and Elizabeth Griffiths of Dudley. There were four other children in the family, William, born 1 July, 1791, Hannah, 30 March, 1793, Elizabeth, 22 February, 1798 and Richard, 11 October, 1802. William, the eldest son was by all accounts a sickly child, and both he and his sister Hannah died young.

1

March 1795

Baptiz:d 8   Mary Daughter of Thomas and Margaret Weydon

8   Mary Daughter of Philip and Isabra Hiller

15 John son of Benjamin and Sarah Haywards

19 Susannah daughter of Josiah and Ann Reynolds   *Foreign*

22 Joseph Son of Benjamin and Ann Seabrook   *Foreign*

22 Mary Daughter of John and Joanna Bidell   *Foreign*

22 Henry Son of John and Ann Baker   *Foreign*

27 Josiah Son of Josiah and Elizabeth Mason

29 Ann Daughter of William and Elizabeth Devey   *Foreign*

29 Susannah daughter of Thomas and Thomas Brooks

March 1   Ann Daughter of William Powell   *Foreign*

5   Elizabeth wife of Thomas Rouse   5th William Steward

7   Eliza Watkins   Foreign   10th Betty Meeke Widow

14 Samuel Son of John Boraston   12th Mary Wells

15 James Green   16th William Son of William Hill

17 Thomas Son of Richard Morris   19th Sarah Bucknell &c

1.   *Entry of baptism of Josiah Mason from Parish Registers,
Kidderminster Parish Church, St. Mary and All Saints.*

His father and grandfather were weavers of a twilled fabric of silk and worsted, called bombazine, but the grandfather was also an inventor, an excellent mechanic in great demand as a repairer of looms, weaving machinery and water mills. The old man was also, by all accounts, something of a humorist, sociable, musical, a good smoker, and very proud and fond of Mason. Mason's mother was described as a clean thrifty kind of woman. Despite all their skills the family lived in relative poverty.

Mason made several attempts to supplement the family income through a variety of enterprises, but without any great or lasting success. At the same time he gained what education he could, at a dame school next door to his home, and at the local Unitarian Sunday school, but also added to this knowledge by his own efforts. Then at the age of 21 years he moved to Birmingham to live with his Uncle, and on the 13 August 1817, at Aston Parish Church he married his cousin Annie Griffiths.(2) Some anecdotal information handed down in the family, says that, Mason was a fiery man, for when he first met his wife she was engaged to someone else, and the story goes that he threw her engagement ring into a river, as he wanted to marry her himself. He obviously succeeded, and the match evidently had parental approval, as his mother, Elizabeth Mason, and Annie's father, Richard Griffiths, were entered as witnesses on the marriage certificate. The couple set up their first home at a small house in Bagot Street.

2. *Entry of marriage of Josiah Mason and Annie Griffiths, Aston Parish Registers, 13th August, 1817.*

Mason worked long and hard and his industrial enterprises prospered, and he was eventually drawn towards philanthropy. Entrepreneurs like Mason who became philanthropists were often recognised by the marked simplicity of their lives; spurning social engagements and spending their money on others rather than themselves, and there were often common belief systems of politics and religion which affected both their industrial enterprise and philanthropic endeavours. Many were inbred with Victorian Liberalism and Protestant Christianity, and were active in Liberal politics. They presented typical models of Victorian businessmen "methodical, regular and thrifty in their habits", relentless in their capacity for hard work and self-improvement, and models of self-discipline and temperance in their personal lifestyles.

How Mason matched up to this description will be considered later. Suffice for the moment to say, that according to Willert Beale, he lived frugally, often on two lamb chops and a glass of water. Beale who wrote a number of articles on Mason in the 1880's was rather scathing of his generosity, indicating that for all his public philanthropy, he did not consider him a generous man. He wrote that he had never heard of him making a spontaneous charitable gift, but had heard of many claims for urgent assistance turned away. It may be, that the acquisition of a fortune from humble beginnings, had made him particularly careful, and discriminating. Even it appears, to the point of bargaining in a drapers shop in Birmingham, when he offered eight pence (3p) for a tie priced at a shilling (5p).

But there is much more to Mason than suggested by the few jaundiced comments above. For his philanthropy increased in scope, and extent, when the British economy was at its most dynamic, between 1850 and 1880, with a noticeable doubling of gross national income, population increase of over 25% and a massive shift of people into the towns. The resulting industrialisation and urbanisation, such as occurred in Birmingham, made it necessary on the whole for the illiterate, sick and poor to depend on charity.

But there were other factors, commonly held, which may have motivated Mason, among them, the fear of social revolution, humanitarian religious concern for poverty and suffering, satisfaction of some psychological or social need or the desire to improve the moral tone of the recipients, or possibly self conscious guilt about the possession of wealth. However, it is easy to criticise Nineteenth Century employers like Mason who may have exploited their workers, and in consequence made life outside work miserable; but a more generous view attempts to recognise qualities in entrepreneurs which went beyond the desire to make money or attain personal power, to a genuine delight in assisting their customers and work people.

Mason was among the minority of industrialists who did not seek power and influence through direct involvement in the public life of Birmingham, maybe he was dissuaded by the allegations of corruption, mismanagement and extravagance. Nonetheless, he met the criteria for a successful Victorian industrialist. That is wealth, nonconformity and philanthropic endeavour, but his unique and controversial traits need to be more adequately assessed. Special reference will be made to his great wealth, his controversial religious views, his rather covert industrial success, the application of entrepreneurial skill to his philanthropy and most important and demanding of all, an examination of his influence and power, through his personal authority and membership of a circle of influential friends and associates.

Chapter 2
Humble Origins and Self Help

The impression gained from biographical accounts is that Mason was the archetypal, "rags-to-riches", self-made man. There is documentary proof that he was the son of a weaver, and supporting evidence that his grandfather was a weaver. However, his father later in his working life took a small step away from his proletarian roots and became a clerk at a local carpet factory.

His early years do appear to have been spent in relative poverty; a situation he tried to remedy by his own efforts. His birth place was a small house on the left hand side of Mill Street, at the foot of the hill leading to Proudcross, Kidderminster, Worcestershire.(3) (4)A plaque (5) on the existing building states that, "In the house which formerly stood here Sir Josiah Mason founder of Mason's Orphanage and Mason Science College, Birmingham was born". At that time Mill Street consisted of a few cottages surrounded by open fields. In 1882 after his death, part of this street was named Josiah Mason Street.

3. *Birthplace of Josiah Mason on left hand side of Mill Street, at foot of hill leading to Proudcross, Kidderminster, Worcestershire.*

6

4. *Existing house on site of Josiah Mason's birthplace, Mill Street, Kidderminster, Worcestershire, 1992.*

5. *Plaque on house - birthplace site. Josiah Mason, Mill Street, Kidderminster, Worcestershire.*

It was from here that he set out at about the age of eight, with cakes and bread rolls, which be bought at 16 to the dozen from the local baker, sold from door to door,(6) and achieved a margin of profit. "Joe's rolls" became famous among his customers, and his mother was called upon to fit up more baskets to meet the demand of the expanding business. But he was not content with just this outlet, the young entrepreneur also took on the task of bagging up copper - which was plentiful among workpeople in the area - for local tradespeople into packets of 5/- = (25p), at a charge of a 1d (½p) per pound. Increased profitability encouraged him into further capital investment, and to his great joy he was able to purchase a donkey called Admiral Rodney (7). With his baskets turned into panniers he now began to sell fruit and vegetables. His mother supported him in his enterprises, and his father offered his advice, which Mason prided himself on using in later life, "Joe theist got a few pence, never let anybody know how much theist got in thee pockets".

6. *Mason as a boy selling bread "Joe's Rolls" from door to door.*

7. *Mason as a boy with donkey "Admiral Rodney" selling fruit and vegetables.*

There is some evidence that the family were an enterprising group. His mother kept a small grocery shop where she was sometimes assisted by Mason. They sold little packets of gunpowder tea, which they purchased at a guinea (£1.05p) a pound, and loaf sugar which cost nearly 6s (30p) a pound. These were sold in ounces and half-ounces to the poor customers including tramps and beggars from a lodging house nearby. The business was a small one, but expanded when a bakehouse was added, and where in addition to selling bread, they cooked Sunday dinners for local people in the hot ovens.

It was during this period that he taught himself to write, and obtained casual employment writing letters, and coloured and plain valentines for less literate people. With the proceeds, he bought books on theology, history and the elementary sciences, but did not permit himself the luxury of novels or other literature. In his enthusiasm to acquire more education and useful practical skills he enrolled at the local Unitarian Sunday School, a well known Kidderminster Old Meeting, formerly Richard Baxter's Chapel. In those days

Sunday Schools provided basic educational opportunities to acquire reading and writing skills, and were for many their only form of education. It is said that Mason's first contact with pens was in the making of quills for the Sunday School teachers, and pupils.

Despite his education, his early entrepreneurial enterprises had a limited success, and at the age of 15 he decided to seek more solid employment; firstly as a shoemaker, based on the knowledge he had gained from an old shoemaker in Mill Street, he had assisted. This enabled him to remain at home and support his brother William, who was in poor health. He made a number of pairs of boots and shoes for Mr. Clymer, the principal shoemaker in Kidderminster, but the business failed, because in his opinion, he used a superior quality leather. He then looked for work outside the home. During the next few years he had a number of jobs including, shopkeeper, baker, carpenter, blacksmith, and house-painter, but finally settled to his father's occupation of carpet weaver at John Broom's, Tinker Hill works. He received a pound a week after the payment of loom rent, and the assistance of a boy. After two years the poor pay and reduced trade appear to have contributed to his decision to move. At the age of 21 he visited his uncle Richard Griffiths in Birmingham and decided to stay in the hope of finding more lucrative employment.

Richard Griffiths was his mother's brother, and this visit at Christmas 1816 was the beginning of his life and work in Birmingham, and he never again returned to live in Kidderminster. Initially he worked as a labourer, moving coal and emptying furnaces at the Aston Flint Glass Works of B. & W. Gibbins in Bagot Street,(8)(9) where his uncle was clerk and manager. His uncle thought highly of Mason and recognised his business acumen, and rewarded him by asking for his help to investigate a jewellery and gilt toy business he had invested in. Trouble had developed between the uncle and the other partner in the business, and whether through Mason's intervention, or not, the partner left Birmingham. His uncle now put Mason in charge of the enterprise and he moved with his wife to live in a house attached to the factory in Legge Street. Such was his uncle's gratitude that he offered him a share in the business. With this incentive, Mason worked hard for six or seven years improving both profitability and productivity. But, according to Mason, in 1822, his uncle, by now his father-in-law, did not keep his promise and arranged without his knowledge to sell the business to a Richard Bakewell, a mathematical instrument maker of Loveday Street, St. Mary's Square.

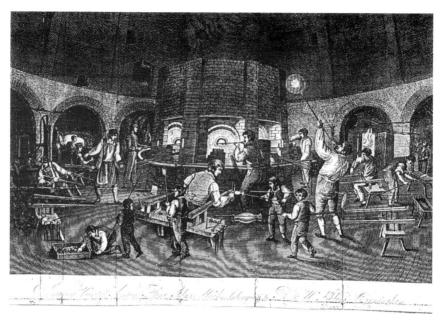

8. *Mason's first work place in Birmingham, The Aston Flint Glass Works of B & W Gibbins in Bagot Street.*

9. *The house in Bagot Street, Birmingham, in which Sir Josiah Mason lived as a young man with his wife Annie.*

Perhaps at this point we are offered a brief insight into Mason's personality. Bunce, his biographer tells how he resolved never to enter his father-in-law's business again, and as a result the business failed, causing Bakewell to commit suicide. Bunce, in the second edition of Mason's biography, issued a correction based on information from Mrs Bakewell, to say that Mason stayed in the company for 18 months after being offered a salary of £300 a year, and Bakewell remained a successful businessman until his death from typhus in 1826.

Unemployment did not suit the active, vigorous 27 year old. The story goes that he met by chance in the street James Heeley, a steel toy maker of Great Charles Street - the Heeleys were an old and respected Birmingham family, and leading Wesleyans. He was a stranger to Mason but he was a member of Belmont Row Chapel and may have known of his unemployment. However, he was anxious to introduce him to Samuel Harrison, a split ring maker, of Lancaster Street, who might be able to offer him employment. When they met, Harrison expressed the opinion that he had met many young men but most were unwilling to dirty their hands. Mason indicated that he was not afraid of hard work and managed to impress Harrison who immediately hired him. This introduction was the turning point in Mason's career, and he invested all his savings of £20 in the business. By extraordinary good fortune Harrison was moving out of his house attached to the workshop to a cottage he had built, and he offered Mason and his wife the tenancy. The house had a pleasant garden and was only a stones throw away from their previous home in Bagot Street and the Belmont Row Chapel they attended.

As usual Mason adapted quickly to his new position as manager of the split ring works. Strangely there was no agreement between the two men regarding remuneration, so for about a year Mason took money from the income of the factory, for living expenses. He then asked Harrison about pay, and Harrison said that he could buy the factory as he wished to retire. Masons's attempts to raise the money failed, but Harrison generously agreed to sell for £500 to be paid from profits, with the first instalment of a £100 to be paid in August 1823, and the last in 1824. Over this time a great friendship developed between the two men which continued until Harrison's death in 1833.

Mason's business was now well developed. The stamping machines had been adapted to produce split rings which had previously been produced by hand, and the production of flat rings - invented by Harrison to hold bunches of keys - was continued. Harrison's inventiveness had also extended to steel pen nibs, called

"Magnum Bonum", probably the first to be produced in Birmingham, they had been made in 1780 for his friend the famous Dr. Priestly. However, Mason was content to expand and develop the split ring business, so that by 1828 the factory had been extended to take in 36, Lancaster Street. With newly constructed machinery to bevel hoop rings - machinery still is use in the factory in 1890 - and improved methods of production his prosperity seemed assured. The improved rings sold for sixpence each so that he was able to make a £1,000 in a single year.

Mason's early initiatives and self-advancement can be considered against the views of Samuel Smiles, who was perhaps one of the greatest advocates of self-help. A philosophy which permeated through nineteenth century society. He proclaimed that "all work which brings honest gain is honourable", and that, "to start in life with comparatively small means seems so necessary as a stimulus to work".

Whether Mason was acquainted with Smiles work is not known, but in laying the foundation stone of his Science College, Mason makes reference to his humble origins and the struggle he had to make his way in the world. Identifying some of the characteristics necessary for success, which were in accord with Smiles on the necessity for perseverance and hard work. An article in Nature commenting on his speech at the ceremony, states that he "gave a simple account of his own career, in which he had amassed a fortune by patient industry, and spoke with great emphasis of the difficulties which he and his comtemporaries had to encounter in their youth from the want of any means of carrying on their education especially in science, during the intervals they had to spare from work".

It is also interesting that the groups Mason helped through his philanthropy were the young, offering self-help through education in science, and older people and orphans for whom self-help offered no practical alternative to their condition.

Chapter 3
Religious Views and Influences

Mason's early years were spent in a traditional Non-conformist household, attending chapel and Sunday school. The chapel, he first attended was Unitarian, and was one of the "Old Dissent" type. Later he moved to the Wesleyan Chapel founded in 1803 near his home in Mill Street.(10)

10. Wesleyan Chapel, Mill Street, Kidderminster, founded 1803 and attended by Mason as a boy and a young man.

When Mason moved to Birmingham in 1824 to stay with his uncle Richard Griffiths he was soon introduced into, and became a member of Belmont Row, Wesleyan Methodist Chapel (11). The chapel, originally called Coleshill Street was built in a poor quarter of Birmingham and had been opened by Wesley in 1790. It afforded Mason the opportunity to make contact with influential members of the Non-conformist business community in Birmingham, which proved invaluable in furthering his career. Non-conformist worship was organised in a very different way from the Church of England, in that the members paid their minister. It was an important difference that gave a caucus of the more well-to-do members of any chapel real authority and commitment, and a knowledge of the spiritual and material well-being of each other in a way that was unknown in the Anglican Church.

11. *Wesleyan Chapel, Belmont Row, Birmingham, attended by the Mason's.*

It has to be remembered that when he became unemployed following the sale of his father-in-law's business, it was James Heeley, a member of Belmont Row Chapel who introduced him to Samuel Harrison a Unitarian, who offered him employment in the split ring works, and eventually sold him the business which formed the basis of his vast industrial empire. It was also through attendance at the chapel that he met G.J. Johnson his legal adviser and mentor, who supported and assisted him throughout his life.

As the Belmont Row Circuit was extended, a chapel was set up in Erdington, and the trustees were some of the more prosperous Birmingham Methodists at Belmont Row, including Richard Griffiths Mason's uncle, and James Heeley. The chapel stood on the site of the present Erdington Fire Station. It was not long before Mason was invited to teach at this Sunday school, which he was more than

willing to do, as it was seen as an important duty by Non-conformists. This action was the beginning of a long association with the
area, where he supported, from time to time, the Wesleyan Methodist
cause, and gained assistance in the development of his wealth. For
in 1835 he leased land north of Penns Lane, near Erdington, from
William Wheelwright, a Methodist, and this was the beginning of his
extensive investment in land. He also became acquainted with
Joseph Webster of Penns, a Unitarian, prominent local industrialist
and landowner, who provided desks and fittings for the Erdington
Methodist Sunday School.

Unfortunately this first chapel at Erdington did not survive, the
trustees had borrowed £500 for building and when they were unable
to discharge the debt in 1823, the Methodist Conference advised
them to sell the building to the Free Episcopalians. However, when
Mason built his first orphanage in 1858 they were able to use a hall
there to resume their activities. Mason's wife, Annie,(12) became a
member of this chapel and he gave £70 to the Circuit Board for what
was practically the chaplaincy of his establishment. When the new
orphanage was completed in 1868 Mason leased land in Station
Road, Erdington for a new church and gave £100 for the cost of
building. Both this church and that of the orphanage were attached
to the Newtown Row Circuit who provided preachers for both establishments. Despite his commitment to Wesleyan Methodism, Mason
had been open to other influences.

12. Annie, Mason's wife.

16

One such involvement was with George Jacob Holyoake, born in Birmingham in 1817. Holyoake had been a Christian until the age of 24, when he heard Robert Owen speaking in Birmingham, and as a result became involved with the Co-operative movement, with its belief in rational religion, and positive human service. Holyoake mentions in his autobiography that "I know one great donor,... one Josiah Mason, who when I and others were advocates of social views in Laurence Street Chapel, used to be one of the hearers". According to Holyoake Mason had an enquiring, observant and ambitious mind, what he termed, "the ambition of usefulness, with self reliance and self-help in him. He knew that thrift was fortune, and when he acquired wealth he opened an orphanage, open to any sect or any race. He had acquired Robert Owen's passion for the formation of character, and that wholesome conditions and good practical education would go a good way towards it in the young - any denomination could conduct services at his orphanage provided they avoided the tenet of eternal punishment.

This appears to be the only reference linking Mason to movements other than Unitarianism and Wesleyan Methodism and giving a hint of socialist leanings in his early years. Their personal relationship developed from Mason's agreement, following a request from Holyoake, to admit, the later infamous, Horatio Bottomley to his orphanage.

As Mason's wealth increased, and he considered philanthropic works, a more individualistic and independent personality showed itself. By his own efforts he set up his first almshouses and orphanage at Sheep Street, Erdington, but soon wanted to make a greater commitment. This was when he outlined the proposals for an orphanage with a £20,000 endowment, in a letter to the Rev. Dr. J.C. Miller, Vicar of Saint Martin's, Birmingham on the 10th November, 1856. Whether Mason was aware of Miller's evangelical views, and belief that the wealthy in society had a God given purpose of improving the lot of those less fortunate, is not known.

Mason's letter was as follows:

Norwood House,
Erdington,

Nov 10 1856

My dear Sir,

I am trustee for various property value about twenty thousand pounds at my own disposal for the benefit of orphans.

I seek advice and help how this could best be worked out either by its own funds or in connection with those willing to further so desirable an object.

My idea is that destitute orphans are the ojbects without reference to class and feel the importance of giving a preference to girls and early training to be fed clothed and a sound plain education and trained up for such purposes as the progressive developments of this allbeit may indicate for their future employment in society. Say two thirds girls, one third boys, half under four years old, some infants.

To be under government inspection and such a committee that would be likely to secure its future wellfair(sic) and the property enrolled in Chancery you have my name but for the present you will kindly consider this private to yourself only.

The few outlines here given I presume to be enough for your present purpose to bring the matter before such persons you may think to consult and after you have gathered from them such ideas they may be disposed to give upon the subject I shall be truly obliged to have the report and a further interview with you.

faithfully yours,

Private

Eventually on 16th March 1857, when Mason was becoming anxious for a reply, he was assured by Miller that his important project had not been forgotten, and that a strictly private meeting of a few select friends was to be called. This delay must have frustrated the enthusiastic and efficient Mason, although there was no hint of this in the correspondence, which continued until the 22nd May 1857, showing a lively discourse between Miller and Mason, supplemented from time to time by other contributors. A letter of the 25th March for instance, referred to some of the other people, Lea, Fowler and Middlemore all prominent in Birmingham life, and members of the Church of England. All correspondence carried pleasantries, expressing pleasure and hope, but remained intransigent on the issue of the catechism, the Church of England clergy insisted be taught in the orphanage. The fundamental disagreement shows deeply held principles, on both sides, which were not to be compromised, and led eventually to Mason's letter of the 22nd May which rounded off the correspondence. His views on religious instruction were made clear, in that he insisted, only scriptural teachings were to be allowed, and as this was not acceptable, Mason concluded, that their support was not forthcoming, and indicated his determination to proceed with the orphanage project alone if necessary.

His opposition is reinforced by an unattributed statement concerning his views on religion, which gave clear indication of Nonconformist opposition to the established Church and Church rates, and a clear disposition towards Evangelicalism and the New Testament.

Further indications of Mason's religious views were given in his discussions with Miller, when he was asked, to what denomination he belonged, he said he could be called 'universal' or 'free'. Miller could not appreciate that he did not belong to any sect. It is not immediately clear what Mason meant to imply by this statement, although this wish to be unfettered by sectarian doctrine was eventually enshrined in the teaching at his orphanage and science college. It should be remembered that other external influences may have been at play, in that the centre of radical agitation in support of Non-sectarian education was in Birmingham.

Mason was faithful to his Non-sectarian principles, and his Nonconformist background by appointing only Protestants to be trustees of the orphanage. He said, "Trustees must also be men holding what are now known as Protestant evangelical doctrines. They must not be members of the Roman Catholic or Unitarian community,.... though at no time can a majority of the trustees belong to any one sect". He went further on doctrinal matters by excluding clergymen - figures who were to be found on the committees of most philanthropic enterprises. He thought "there are no class of men who are such bad hands in the management of property as ministers of religion, and naturally so, for as far as the teaching of the new testament was concerned it was evidently never intended that they should meddle in secular matters". He also felt that, "a number of state church ministers, and dissenting ministers are not likely to work long in harmony together, as long as one section of the Church of Christ is living in a sinful and adulterous connection with the State".

The strongest clue as to the origins of the detached nature of his thinking may perhaps be found in the fierceness of the national debate over education - particularly since both the orphanage and college were educational institutions. The lack of progress towards a national policy may have helped to drive him towards greater non-sectarian independence. His experience of clergymen and money, in the matter of the Anglican Church Rates controversy, when many Non-conformists protested at having to pay for something from which they derived no benefit, may have determined him never to have them on the management of either institution.

Chapter 4
Milestones on the Road to Success

When considering the factors which motivated Mason in life, business and philanthropy, it seems appropriate to examine some important struggles, and events in his life. Poverty, for instance, could have been a great stimulus which developed his entrepreneurial skills, encouraged activities which produced wealth, and coupled with his struggle to gain an education may have increased his determination to succeed. In addition the influence of the Unitarians and Wesleyan Methodists through their Sunday school movement, offered opportunities to learn to read and write, which opened the door to self advancement.

Once Mason began to accumulate wealth, the drive to become wealthy for its own sake was less acute, as were the pursuits of social and political status and power. In fact, he never appeared to crave a high public profile. Other incentives to perpetuate the dynasty and family name, seemed less acute, because they had no children. Although he virtually adopted his great nephew, Josiah Martyn Smith, who became a major legatee of his estate.

There may also have been another attempt during the 1850's to obtain an heir: when he wished to adopt a young boy called Arthur Harris. Arthur's father, John Harris a metallurgist at the Birmingham Mint, had died, at the age of 30, and Mason tried to persuade the widowed mother to agree to the adoption by offering a financial inducement, but the offer was refused much to Mason's annoyance. There was thought to have been some family connection between the Mason and Harris families. Unfortunately for all concerned Arthur died of a heart condition at the age of 18. All this and the absence of immediate family, may have driven him to draw satisfaction from lavishing his attention and wealth on his philanthropic works.

The above events may have sharpened his personal resolve to undertake philanthropy, but there were also other more immediate pressures. Primary among them the constant presence of beggars who accosted him wherever he went, and for who he kept a supply of coins in his pocket which had to be constantly replenished. He often mentioned these encounters. One story he told was of a blind man and his guide. The blind man, so it was said, had found a job in

Liverpool, but had no money to get there. Mason gave them a half sovereign to cover the fare, but was surprised to see them next day, drunk in Birmingham. On another occasion he thought his generosity was being abused when a woman claimed to have been recently discharged from hospital visited his office. His foreman informed him that the woman had visited before in a number of different disguises. When he asked the foreman to examine her bandaged legs she ran off. These incidents convinced Mason that indiscriminate charitable giving was ineffective.

13. Mason surrounded by signs of his achievements.

A contemporary of Mason's a phrenologist called Professor L.W. Fowler, had his own version of the reasons for Mason's success. When he examined his head in 1862 he found it had a circumference of 24 inches, which he said meant that, the strong qualities of his brain were so active that they thoroughly monopolised his whole mind. It also indicated his fondness for children,(13) a strong independent streak, firmness and perceptive qualities, so that his defects are less apparent. A further examination in 1880 confirmed the continued existence of great powers. It is possible that these findings pleased Mason, as phrenology was held in some regard at the time. Although the title of professor gave no greater standing to the findings, as it was assumed by many such practitioners.

However well motivated and able Mason appeared the pressure and stress of his successful advancement may well have taken its toll. In 1841, he suffered a long and mysterious illness of the stomach which resulted in a total loss of energy. He consulted the best medical men in Birmingham, but without success. So in July 1841 he travelled to Paris to seek the advice of the leading French practitioners. Seeing first Dr. Louis, then Dr. Gaudet and finally the very eminent M. Franconneau Dufrene. They agreed in their diagnosis of a gastric condition, but differed as to whether this was complicated by a heart condition. They were also at variance as to treatment, agreeing only that external applications and taking the waters at Vichy would be beneficial, but disagreed as to whether he should be bled copiously. With all this advice and treatment he did not improve so decided to return to England and take the water cure at Malvern under Dr. Gully.

Friends tried to dissuade Mason from taking this treatment, but without success, for in December 1841 when he felt an attack coming on he travelled to Malvern arriving on the 26th. He stayed until February when he wrote the following:-

"In leaving Malvern for a time it gives me much pleasure to be able to do so with my health considerably improved for the better, and in the hope of it being totally restored. After many years exertion of my brain in business, my health failed. I became subject to attacks of a serious kind, in which my nervous system was so completely destroyed and shattered that I could not bear the slightest noise or light, without excruciating agony. At such times my strength utterly left me. For several of these seizures, I was treated by the first medical men in Birmingham who tried all kinds of medicine, but I could never take more than the first two or three

drops without symptoms which alarmed my medical atten-
dant. My complaints were said to be caused by inflammation
of the mucous membrane of the stomach. Between attacks I
never felt well, my head was all confusion, my spirits often
miserably low, and all attention to business was a pain to me.

By medical advice I tried travelling and went to Paris,
consulted doctors who advised warm baths and drink Vichy
water, from both I derived benefit. However, they did not
keep off the serious attacks. In December, feeling an attack
coming on, decided not to try remedies. Decided to try
waters although friends prophesied death if I did so. I went
to Malvern under the care of Dr. Wilson and Dr. Gully on the
26th of December, having all the symptoms in the worst
degree. After four weeks treatment with a feeling of health
not known for several years. My appetite grew, and I could
walk ten or twelve miles per day, four or five before break-
fast. I continued with the treatment until the middle of
February. Physic did more harm than good".

Unfortunately a few years later the pressures of business again
appeared to have weighed heavily on Mason, and he and his wife
Annie, embarked on a trip of "relaxation". In November 1847, they
set sail for Ostend, from where they travelled to Brussels, bought a
carriage and drove leisurely to Paris. When he arrived at the station
in Paris to catch the train to Tours, he missed it by a fine margin as
the gates were closed just as he arrived. The train was involved in an
accident and many of the passengers were killed. He often retold
this story and indicated that he never again felt annoyed when
delayed, as he thought it was designed for his protection. This story
is corroborated in hand written notes left by a relative - who refers
to the Masons as uncle and aunt - and adds that this was the first
time in their married life that Aunt Mason was ever unpunctual.

Continuing on the "Grand Tour" they reached Tours, and then
on bad roads to Bordeaux. The journey seems to have been particularly difficult, needing at times eight horses and two bullocks to
pull the carriage, providing to Mason's delight an almost royal procession. They continued on to Toulon and Marseilles and then by sea to
Italy, where he visited Bologna, Naples, Florence and Rome - where
he saw the carnival, in March 1848 - as revolution broke out. During
his travels he acquired a number of works of art in bronze, gold and
silver intending to use them in the electroplating business. Unfortunately, many of them were lost when an agent died in Naples, and
his property was seized by the government. He had intended to

travel to Egypt and sail up the Nile, but he felt the need to return to his business in England, and appears never to have travelled abroad again.

In fact, from then on most of his time seems to have been spent in Birmingham. But the Birmingham, of that period, was not only an industrial centre, it was also the hub of the commercial life of the mining district of South Staffordshire, providing services and trading facilities of a widening region, founded on the iron and coal of the "Black Country".

The town had a industrial structure which gave rise to some interesting theories, related to the size of units of production. According to these theories, most people worked in small workshops employing four or five men, particularly in trades such as gun making and jewellery, and this was said to have contributed to good industrial relations in Birmingham. Unfortunately it also led to the role of the factory being underplayed, and underestimated. Factories were very much in existence, Bore estimated that 12 firms, including that of Mason, were engaged in the pen manufacturing trade in Birmingham, employed between them about 3,000 women and girls, and 600 men and boys and that by 1881 93% of the pen-makers of England and Wales were located in Birmingham. These factories were well established, and assured of a continued existence because of the buoyant industrial base, which produced great wealth for some, but conditions of poverty and deprivation for others.

This was the buoyant industrial background - accompanied by religious and political controversy surfacing in the Non-conformist opposition to Church Rates, the Catholic question and expanding Methodism - against which Mason developed his industrial and philanthropic enterprises. A town which developed a reputation at home and abroad for quality products and effective local government, epitomised by the advent of the "civic gospel", a locally developed approach to encouraging people into public life on the basis of moral responsibility, and high ethical standards.

It is appropriate here to consider Mason in relation to his industrial enterprises, in which he fulfilled, in common with many entrepreneurs of the period, the role of capitalist, financier, works manager, merchant and salesman. This required a whole range of talents, the most significant of which was an almost obsessive dedication to work. His friend Johnson relates how Mason visited his solicitor Palmer in his lunch hour dressed in his work clothes to save time, and as if to further emphasise his commitment, relates how after his marriage ceremony and a meal of cold meat and bread he returned as usual to work. Johnson ends, "Josiah Mason was one of those men who could not help getting money. His large brain, enormous power of work and simple habits gave him great advantages over the majority of his fellows". His natural talents and ability to be both innovative and to build upon the ideas of others, gave his vast pen-nib empire its initial boost. First his improvement to existing steel pen-nibs, and subsequently production on a large scale under contract to Perry and Co., the major providers in the country.

Despite inventive talents only three patents were found registered in his name. This may indicate that his strengths lay in determining the goods to be offered for sale, setting the price and confirming the market to be served. It was certainly Mason who having put capital into Elkington & Co., moved them away from the expensive manufacture of electro-plated works of art, such as Greek vases, to the mass market of knives and forks.

Chapter 5
Penmaking

The steel pen replaced the quill in about 1803, and the trade grew because of technical advances in the 1820's. Both the general expansion of trade and the spread of education in the nineteenth century caused a great increase in the amount of writing, and the demand for writing materials. The supply of quill pens would have been seriously constrained if it had not been supplemented by the manufacture of steel pens, at cheap prices, and in quantities which could be indefinitely increased.

A large proportion of the trade was centred, in about 8 main firms in Birmingham, of which three claimed to have originated or perfected technical advances. They all produced on a large scale, eventually employing over a thousand people including several hundred female workers on presswork. Often there were related trades carried out at the same factory, such as small metalwares, like paper clips, and ink stands.

James Perry was the leading manufacturer in the country, and had improved the pen with his patents of 1832 and 1836, introducing a hole in the nib just above the split. The virtues of these 'Perryian Pens", were that they compared favourably with the softness of the quill, because of the patented features of aperture and split.

This design was in advance of Mitchell, Gillott and Mason in Birmingham, but Perry's pens differed from theirs in not being entirely machine made. The balance of evidence tends to support the fact, that steel pens were first made by mechanical means using tools worked by a screw press around 1830, and that the names associated with this method of manufacture were John Mitchell, Joseph Gillott and Josiah Mason each contributing in his own way something towards perfecting the process.

Mason was making steel barrel pens in small quantities in 1827, slip pens in 1828 and was the first person to make cedar penholders. Then in 1829 he spotted nine slip pens on a card for sale in Peart's Bookshop, Bull Street, Birmingham at three shillings and sixpence (17.5p) each. When he saw Peart using one he was sure that he could improve on this standard pen, so he persuaded him to sell the one he was using. By spending hours that night he was able to produce three pens. He sent these to the address on the pen. Perry, Red Lion Square, London. Perry was so impressed that he travelled to 36, Lancaster Street arriving two days later at eight o'clock in the morning to discuss production. So began the arrangement which lasted for 46 years, of Mason being the sole producer of Perryian Pens.(14) Initially there were 12 people employed at the factory, but production grew over the years, from 20 gross in 1829 to 100 gross in 1830 and by 1831 the value of pens produced was £1,421. The growth was due in part to the fact that Mason was able to reduce prices, and with increased literacy demand grew. This called for increased investment in machinery and manpower, until Mason became the largest producer and employer in the penmaking industry.

14. Perry & Co., pen-nibs on display at the Birmingham Museum of Science and Industry - manufactured by Mason.

He became self-sufficient buying steel from Sheffield, and reducing it to the required thickness. His machines were made under supervision by John Drane of Birmingham. However, part of the process of slitting nibs up to the shank, by means of a press, without splitting it or causing the points to overlap, as opposed to cracking with a hammer, was kept a secret by Mason. This was one of his specific contributions to Victorian technology. (15)

Once the steel pen trade had overcome the prejudice against the use of its products from people who preferred reed or goose quill pens, trade began to expand, so that by 1848 it had developed into an important industry, with increased production from 65,000 gross weekly in 1849, to 98,000 gross weekly 15 years later.

Up to 1850 a firm at Oldbury had supplied the Birmingham pen-makers with steel strip, but that market had been lost to Sheffield. The production of pen-nib blanks from the steel strip with a hand press was well known, but the mechanical slitting process was still kept secret by Gillott and Mason. Drane the machine manufacturer tried to copy their technique without having knowledge of the whole process, and failed. It was around this time, according to Mason, that Gillott suggested they become partners, but he refused, although he went on to manufacture pens for him.

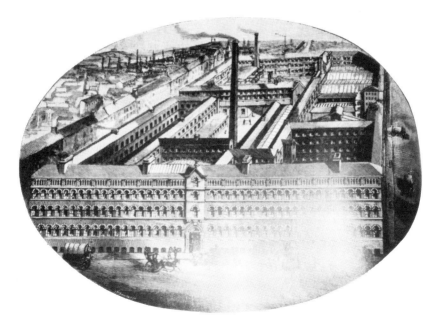

15. Lancaster Street, Birmingham, Mason's Pen Works.

Rolling the Steel.

Piercing.

CUTTING BLANKS

Raising or Shaping.

Hardening.

STAMPING.

SLITTING ROOM,

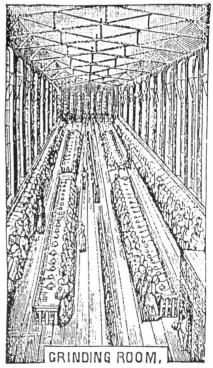

GRINDING ROOM,

31

Grinding.

Scouring or Barreling.

16. Sketches of pen making process.

The manufacturers were able to use semi-skilled labour for most processes, (16) mostly women and girls, but they had to employ one group of very specialised tookmakers who by all accounts had to be trained from boyhood. This meant that only large manufacturers could afford to provide such training. Another special feature of the industry was an almost total absence of sub-contracting except for "carders" - women who took pens home from the factory and sewed them onto cards. These "foggers" as they were sometimes called had numbers of girls working for them - in one instance recorded, there were eleven. In the 1880's attempts were made by Joseph Tanner, the Marxist of the Social Democratic Federation, and others, to organise the women pen workers. It appears that Tanner gave up his job to organise them, and to continue the never ending campaign against sweating in the Birmingham trades. It appears that he had met with some success by 1889.

It was Mason's practice to produce pens with his customers names on, which contributed to him being little known outside Birmingham. This anonymity continued despite the fact that he became one of the foremost pen manufacturers in the world and was the sole maker of the Persian and steel B. pens sold under the Perry name. Locally he contracted with Somerville & Co., from 1851, until 1870 when he purchased the business, but continued to trade under the old name.

An interestin, but little know fact, was that G.R. Elkington, with whom Mason was in partnership in the electroplating industry, was also involved for a time in the pen trade. A handwritten note from Martyn J. Smith, Mason's great nephew stated that, "Bunce does not seem to have known of Mr. Elkington's association with Mason in this industry, or that the pen works at Lancaster Street were at one time purchased by Mr. G.R. Elkington and bought back again by my late uncle. I enclose a few pens marked G.R. Elkington, Birmingham, produced when pen works Mr. Elkington's property".

According to the Elkington archive the pen-nib partnership between Mason and G.R. Elkington was dissolved on 26 May, 1852 after they had been trading in steel pens together, for some time, at Lancaster Street. This was because Mason was keen to trade again on his own account. The record states that there had been no stock-taking or valuation since the previous Christmas, but it was agreed that Mason pay £1,100 to Elkington within four months.

Mason's pen manufacture expanded under the management of Stephen Samsun, formerly his foreman, when weekly production rose by between eight and ten gross. Samsun, like many others in the industry, was inventive and obtained a patent for pen-holders registered in 1861. Later Samsun left the business to work in France for another pen manufacturer A. Somerville and Co., but it appears that he retained the link with Mason and introduced his pen-nibs on the Continent. Demand continued to grow taking in both the European and American market so that the business became an enormous undertaking.

Mason's business continued to prosper, and in 1852, Isaac Smith, his nephew, became manager. He and his brother William had worked for Mason's brother Richard in the split ring business, given him by Mason. When Richard died in 1846 they continued to work for Mason. However, Isaac had been apprenticed to pen making with William Mitchell, and now put his skills to good use and by 1858 the factory had to be extended. It was also apparent that new muffles were required. Muffles were box like containers which separate products from combustion in a furnace, and were very important in pen-making. Mason himself had invented a rotary muffle which proved very effective when the business was small, but as production increased following Isaac Smith's involvement, they needed replacing. Smith decided to use Otto Siemen's gas generators, and Siemen supervised the building of the new muffles, and demonstrated their use in pen-making.

Mason was always interested in improving his manufacturing processes, for which he was praised by Dr. G.W. Siemens in a lecture at the Midland Institute on 20 October 1881 - after Mason's death. He referred to the way Mason and George Elkington used electricity in the 1840's when it was only a philosophers delight, and how Mason had given Siemen his first opportunity by adopting in 1843 his improvements to the electroplating process, and the opportunity in 1871 of improving production in the pen industry.

When Isaac Smith died in 1868, W.F. Batho took over management of the pen-works. He was involved in a major way in all Mason's enterprises, including eventually the Science College. William Fothergill Batho was born at Salford on 11 January 1828. He was manager of Messrs. Peyton and Peyton's tube works Birmingham and from 1866 to 1870 was manager of Messrs. Nettlefold and Company, until be became managing partner of the pen-works.

But in 1871 Batho left the pen-works to allow Mason to resume control on the completion of his orphanage. Mason in his customary way began to expand the business through the purchase of A. Somerville and Co., not from Somerville - who was abroad - but Pollack who was in charge of the business. He was encouraged to attempt to increase output to 40,000 gross per week, but by 1875 he was only able to achieve 32,000 gross. This is perhaps not too surprising as it was the beginning of the so called "Great Depression", which continued for some years. It was at this time - prior to the takeover by the company formed under the Perry & Co., Limited title - that the business was passed to the Trustees who traded under the name of Perry and Co. By this time the Lancaster Street works had grown so that the buildings mostly five storeys high covered two acres, and were described by Mason in 1875 as the largest pen factory in the world.

In the midst of all this Mason showed his continued inventiveness by producing a patent for a new box which held a gross of pen-nibs. They were used to introduce a range of nibs, and each box was marked with the nib-number. He also turned his attention to the nibs, as the following article in the Engineer of 3 June 1870 records, "Mr. Josiah Mason, of the firm of Elkington and Mason, who has a pen factory on his own account, has recently introduced a metallic pen which provides the much-felt want of a double prop for the nibs in the up strokes when writing.

Apparently Mason made hundreds of different pen-nibs, numbered and categorised as fine, medium etc., Philip Poole, a London pen dealer, has in his possession what appear to be traveller's samples of Mason's nibs. (17) They are laid out in rows on a roll, in nib types and numbers, e.g. raven black, manufactured Mason 1829, Elkington & Mason, electro gill, and Grey steel pens. (18) After these various partnership, and before he retired, Mason began to manufacture pen-nibs under his own name, which led people to believe that there was a new manufacturer in the field.

17. Mason pen-nib samples roll showing rare Elkington & Mason nibs.

As production continued to increase Mason became a large employer of labour amounting in 1870 - when production of steel pens was 100,000 gross weekly, using 10 tons of steel - to over a 1,000 employees. This was a large enterprise when seen against the total population of Birmingham of 1871 of 343,786 of whom 167,636 were male and 176,151 female. A short paragraph in the "Gossip" column of the Ironmonger, for 31 October 1867, illustrates this point and states, "Steel-pen manufacturers in Birmingham employ 380 men and 2,000 women and girls; 98,000 gross of pens are turned out weekly, in which ten tons of steel, worth £3,000, are used. Thirty years ago these pens were sold at 5s. per gross, they now bring only 1½d. to 1¾d.

By the time Mason retired, at the age of eighty, 60 tons of pens equal to one and a half million pens per ton were in process through the factory. It was now an enormous undertaking employing about a thousand workers four fifths of whom were women.

Some indication of how Mason provided for his employees was shown when the factory inspector, J.E. White, reported on Mason's

𝔚𝔥𝔬𝔩𝔢𝔰𝔞𝔩𝔢 𝔓𝔯𝔦𝔠𝔢 𝔏𝔦𝔰𝔱

OF

MERCANTILE PENS,

MANUFACTURED BY

SIR JOSIAH MASON,
36, LANCASTER STREET,
BIRMINGHAM.

No.	POINTS.	NAME AND DESCRIPTION.	℔ GROSS. s.	d.
A1	Ex. Fine	Patent Ink Regulator Pen	2	0
A2	Fine	„ „ „	2	0
A3	Medium	„ „ „	2	0
A4	Broad	„ „ „	2	0
102	Fine	Ready Writer	0	9
103	Medium	„ „	0	9
107	Fine	Rib Pen	1	0
117	Fine	Three Hole Correspondence Pen	1	0
121	Ex. Fine	Universal Office Pen	1	0
122	Fine	„ „ „	1	0
126	Ex. Fine	Banker's Posting Pen, Extra Strong	1	4
132	Fine	Ladies' Fountain Pen	1	0
133	Medium	„ „ „	1	0
137	Fine	Falcon Shell Fish Pen	0	10
202	Fine	Grey Shoulder Pen	1	0
207	Fine	Curve Point Pen	1	0
212	Fine	Embossed A Pen	1	0
217	Fine	„ B „	1	0
222	Fine	„ D „	1	2
229	Broad	„ J „	1	2
277	Fine	„ G „	1	2
232	Fine	Adamant Pen, Triangle	1	6
237	Fine	Turned Up Point	1	4
251	Ex. Fine	Counting House Pen	1	4
252	Fine	„ „ „	1	4
253	Medium	„ „ „	1	4
256	Ex. Fine	Antique Pen	1	6
257	Fine	„ „	1	6
258	Medium	„ „	1	6
263	Medium	Solicitor's Pen	1	4
264	Broad	„ „	1	4
267	Fine	Five Slit Bank Pen	1	6
272	Fine	Best Swan Pen	1	4
282	Fine	Elastic Swan Quill	1	6
283	Medium	„ „ „	1	6

18. Sir Josiah Mason pens price list.

36

19. Plan of Lancaster Street Pen Works.

Lancaster Street pen factory,(19) in 1864. He said, "This factory shows that much can be done towards securing healthy work places, even under unfavourable circumstances. It fronts on the street in a crowded and poor part of the town, but care has been taken to provide the best modes of ventilation in the workshops, and also up the main staircase, closets free from smell, &c. The "twice divided" shafts of Mure, i.e. with four actual divisions, so as to secure an up and down current of air from whatever quarter the wind sets. A marked improvement has been found in the health of the females engaged in one of the shops, in which a dusty process is carried on, since these means have been adopted. More space has lately been secured, and further improvements are being carried out. Guards are used to protect the workers from the flying oil and dust , and some machinery under the benches is guarded. In some shops all or most were women, their strength or skill being needed, any younger being no profit; a man in charge of one shop liking married women best, 'not a lot of giddling girls'."

The report continues with interviews with some of the children employed by Mason. The first was Henry Warner, he said, "Roll steel, as do two other boys. Get 4s.6d. a week. Mother saves me 6d. out of it, and buys me trousers. Can read (can). Learned by going to school for about half a year while in a factory at Tutbury. Could not read at all before, and have never been to a day or night school since, but go on Sunday. Cannot write. Christ was him that died on the cross for us, to make us go to Him".

Next was Samuel Enfield, age 10y. 11m., "Here nearly 4 years. Lacquer pens, turning them in a barrel by a handle. Worked at umbrellas before, and went there when going 7. The hours were from 8 to 7, but sometimes till 8. Got 9d. a week at first, and then 1s. Was the youngest there. Was at day school 12 months, and go on Sunday, but cannot at night because I stay here till 8". Then Thomas Whitehouse, age 13. "At day school a month once. Don't go on Sunday. Cannot spell 'i-s'. Know some of my letters. Been at this and wire work since 9 years old".

The questioning continued with Charles Walkers, age 10. "Harden pens. Fill pans, and about every half hour for 5 minutes pull them out of the muffle with an iron, and help the man. The hours are from 7a.m. till 8p.m.; but on Monday and Friday only till 7, and on Saturday till 1. Get 4s. a week. Was at gun work before, and minded a machine. Was at day school a year, and have been on Sunday. Can read the Testament, but not do sums. Cannot read 'doubt'. The minister is him as preaches at church". Then Mary Saunders was interviewed, "Have bobbed steel on a wheel for nine years. Am 25 now. Wear the brown paper over my apron to keep the sparks off. Sometimes they burn it, and my apron strings too. Feel stuffed up in the chest, and have a cough". [Note. There is a constant stream of sparks, not, however, warm to the touch. The steel dust lies on the folds of the brown paper, &c.] When Charlotte

Woodcock, age 14 was interviewed, she said, "Cut strips of steel with a rotary plane, worked by the steam. Get 3s.6d. a week. Was never at a day or night school, but go on Sunday now and then. Father or mother never said anything about school to me. Don't know 'S' or 'N' ".

Sarah Ann Wedge, age 12 then took her turn, "Was at school ever since mother could see us reach the top of the stool, when we was little children. Can read, write and sum. One sum was 'Dictation'. Am sure". [Note - Very tidy and happy looking. Parents well off.] The interviews continued with Martha Sarty, age 17, "Always have the same hours of work. Get 7s.6d. a week. Went to buttons at ten years old. Can hardly remember what I did at school. Can read, but not if the words are hard, and cannot write. Go to school on Sunday, sometimes; never to night school". The next person was Eliza Bashford, age 14, "Pierce lids of paper boxes with a press, to fasten a pen in as a pattern. My finger is hurt from pinching it, by my letting the fly drop. Did so once before. Can read the Bible, and write, but not very well. Read about Joseph and Abraham, and Isaac, and all those. Was at school till going 14, and paid 3d. a week".

The last young person to be questioned was Jane Lury, age 14, "Never was at school till I came to the warehouse here, and could scarcely read at all. The woman under whom I work, got me to go to school four nights a week for 2d. I can now read, write and spell". [Note. These pains were taken because the girl's appearance betokened good capacity.]

There was also some indication of how Mason felt about the hours they worked, for he asked Henry Bore to write to Sir James Ferguson, Secretary of the Royal Commission as follows:-

Sir,   *Birmingham, June 11, 1875.*

I am directed by Sir Josiah Mason to state that he would prefer the hours of labour in the Factory Act remaining as they are. There are about 700 hands subject to the Act employed at these works, and I believe that the majority of these hands would object to any alteration in the hours. The hands under the Act work 50 hours per week (from 8 o'clock to 6) I have had the carrying out of the Act in these works since its application, and can testify that the hands earn as much money, and that there is as much work done as under the old system of 59 hours.

I am, &c.   *Pro Sir Josiah Mason,*
                                         Henry Bore.

As the businesses in the Birmingham pen trade became more inter-connected and dependent upon each other, some local men of eminence decided in conjunction with some of the leading proprietors to establish a limited company, by amalgamating the various firms under the Perry & Co. Limited title.

Soon after the takeover process began, the Ironmonger of 1 April 1876 recorded:- "Perry & Co., Ltd., The company has been registered, with a capital of £500,000 in £10 shares, to take over the business and properties of three well known London and Birmingham firms. The objects are thus defined:- To purchase the business of split ring, pen and penholder manufacturer and merchant carried on by Sir Josiah Mason, in his own name and under the style of A. Somerville and Co., at the Perryian or Lancaster Street Pen Works, Lancaster Street, Birmingham. The company will acquire all the plant, machinery and other property connected therewith. Also to purchase the business of gold pen, pencil, pencil case, percussion cap, cartridge and ammunition manufacturers, and brassworks carried on by Messrs W.E. Wiley, under the style of Wiley and Son, in Graham Street, Birmingham, together with all property appertaining thereto.. Also to purchase the business of Messrs. J.J. Perry and L.H. Perry of 37, Red Lion Square and 3, Cheapside, London, trading as pen merchants, pencil, elastic band, and ink manufacturers, and dealers in stationers' sundries, under the style of James Perry & Co., together with all the effects of the said business. An agreement regulates the purchase of the business and property of Messrs. Wiley & Son, the consideration being £36,000, payable in fully paid shares". (20)

A meeting of the promoters of the new company met on the 19 November, 1897 at 15, Colmore Row, Birmingham and elected Joseph Henry Nettlefold as chairman and Howard C. Parkes as secretary. The minutes make interesting reading as they give some detail of the formation of Perry & Co., Limited, and some of the trials and tribulations of the directors in their negotiations with the separate companies. They appointed Quilter Ball & Co., to report on each company in turn, and when Wilton of that company presented his information on Mason's business they resolved to revise their original offer of £130,000 down to £115,000. This offer was put to Mason's solicitors Tyndall, Johnson & Tyndall, and in addition, it was agreed that the committee should meet with Mason. However, the solicitors replied to the effect that it was useless to think that Mason would accept a reduction. The chairman then proposed that Mason take the difference of £30,000 in 5% preference shares, and this was agreed.

347.72
PE 876/2

PERRY & COMPANY, LIMITED
CAPITAL,
£500,000 IN 50,000 SHARES OF £10 EACH

Directors,

Joseph Henry Nettlefold, Chairman,
John Curtland,
Francis Atkins,

Joseph John Perry } Managing
William Edward Wiley } Directors
Maurice Pollack, Secretary.

The Perryian & Lancaster Street Works,
Birmingham, February 1st 1876

Dear Sir,

Having purchased for the purpose of amalgamation and extension the businesses of

Sir Josiah Mason
A. Sommerville & Co. } 36, Lancaster Street, Birmingham
Perry & Co., 37, Red Lion Square & 3, Cheapside, London
W. E. Wiley & Son, Graham Street, Birmingham

all of which Businesses will be carried on in the same manner as hitherto, we beg to solicit the continuance of your favours to which the increased facilities at our command, will enable us to pay the strictest and most immediate attention.

We remain, Sir,
Your obedient Servants,
Perry & Co. Limited.

P.S.—

We request you to address your communications to the respective departments thus:—

Perry & Co., Limited, Sir Josiah Mason, 36, Lancaster Street, Birmingham

Perry & Co., Limited, A. Sommerville & Co., 36, Lancaster Street, Birmingham

Perry & Co. Limited, 37, Red Lion Square, London.

Perry & Co., Limited, W. E. Wiley & Son, Graham Street, Birmingham.

20. Perry & Co. Ltd., *notice to customers following amalgamation of customers.*

41

Difficulties were then experienced with Somerville & Co., part of Mason's enterprise. It appeared that Mason had a £1,000 security bond from Somerville's deposited with the Birmingham Banking Company which he wished the new company to take over, but they wanted this to be part of the £30,000. There was also a dispute over the stock with the wish to value pens marked Sir Josiah Mason as good, and those marked Josiah Mason doubtful. Parkes also produced a statement of Somerville's and Mason's bad debts, and the committee resolved that they wished to receive £389 from Mason in settlement, excluding the good debts of £1,576.0.4 which were to be guaranteed by Pollack, as manager of Mason's business, and then transferred to the Company. But Mason's troubles were not over on 14 December 1875, the committee asked Perry to allocate two of his workers to take stock of Mason's company, as they did not wish to make their agreement with him null and void. When they met again on the 28 December the signing of the cheque to purchase was again postponed, until the 31st. Then a cheque for a £20,000 deposit was signed for Mason's business including Somerville's.

Then on the 1 January 1876, Pollack and the managers of the various departments of Mason's business were called in to be told that the purchase had gone through, and it was hoped that they would be willing to work for the new company under Joseph J. Perry, who had been appointed Managing Commercial Director, and W.E. Wiley as Managing Director of the manufacturing department.

It was at this point that Mason made a request to the Board to use his private office at Lancaster Street, between 10a.m. and 1p.m. each day. An unusual request when Mason was only a month away from his 81st birthday. However, this was agreed subject to it not being required by the Company. Mason's nephew Martyn Smith also asked if he could remain with the company, but requested a salary of £400 a year, this was agreed and he was appointed Manager of the Lancaster Street Works.

However, by the 11 January, 1876, the negotiations with the other companies had been broken off, and it was decided not to use the Perry & Co. Ltd. title for the new company, but to call it "Sir Josiah Mason's Company Limited". Shortly afterwards it was agreed to resume its use, and bank accounts were opened at the Joint Stock Bank on behalf of Perry & Co. Ltd..

The stocktaking at Lancaster Street met with some difficulties, which involved Mason personally. Wiley reported to the board that

Mason had removed large quantities of pens from the factory to his private residence. Mason's response was to say that the pens were for his personal use in the orphanage, and that in any case they had been classified as class B, for which the Company were only willing to pay 4d. a gross. The chairman indicated that he would investigage the matter through the solicitors, but he later reported that he felt it more judicious to let the matter, "remain for a little time". But Pollack reported that Mason had removed the pens prior to stock-taking, and that they were not very saleable, but the Chairman Nettlefold was not convinced, and said that Mason should not have removed anything.

There were also difficulties over fixing the purchase price of Mason's business because of disagreement over the valuation of the stock. The secretary said that the businesses purchased by the Company had been carried on in the usual way and that sales had been little affected by the bad state of trade.

With regard to the business of A. Somerville, Mason had to pay debts up to 30 November, 1875, and arrangements regarding lease-holds etc., were to be passed to Perry & Co. for £1,000, and trade marks had also to be transferred. Mason had deposited, with the Birmingham Banking Company, certain documents as security for repayment to Alfred Somerville.

Mason wanted this business to begin on 30 November, 1875, so arranged that he, James Gibbs Blake and George James Johnson should be trustees for the company about to be formed, and for the parent company to succeed as from 1 January, 1876. It was agreed that Gibbs Blake, Bunce, Heslop, Johnson and George Shaw should hold £25,000 of the Lancaster Street properties.

Finally, in February 1877 the businesses of Sir Josiah Mason, James Perry & Co. and W.E.Wiley & Son were purchased with the foreign businesses of Joseph J. Perry and J. Perry & Co. of Brussels and New York, and their business interests in Amsterdam and Frankfurt.

Around 1919 Perry & Co. divided into two, with the two Perry brothers going their separate ways; J.J. Perry remained in Birming-ham producing pen nibs, while Edmund Stephen Perry moved to Edmonton, London. Then in 1956 the Company moved to Gosport, still produced, among other things, steel pen nibs, but were not able to use the Perry name so traded under the name Iridinoid, from 1959-60, then began to produce fountain pens and primary school teaching aids and changed their name to Osmiroid, Berol, of Kings Lynn, took over in 1990, closed the Gosport factory and moved to

Kings Lynn. The part of Perry & Co. which had remained in Birmingham, later diversified their manufacture into other engineering goods, producing jacks, needles and sinkers for the textile trade, as the process was similar to that used for stamping out steel pens. They remained in existence until 1953, when the engineering part of the business was taken over by Renolds Coventry Chain, a Birmingham company who now operate from Manchester, and the pen-nib part by British Pens, with John O. M. Smith, a relative of Mason's as Director.

Chapter 6
Enterprise in Partnership

Although Mason's name is most strongly linked with pen manufacture, he also had other business interests. One of these was his investment in the electroplating industry. He had sold his house Woodbrooke in 1839 to George Richard Elkington who with his cousin Henry had pioneered the commercial application of the process. The Elkingtons had struggled for some time with the difficult task of coating metals. But in 1840 they made some advance and successfully applied for a patent.

Up until 1840 the method of applying silver onto copper was done by hand by Boulton and Watt at the Soho Works, and later by Sir Edward Thomason and other manufacturers, a slow and costly process. But John Wright, a Birmingham surgeon, discovered in 1840, a way electricity could take silver and spread it evenly and firmly over base metals. This enabled the Elkingtons with Alexander Parkes, an able inventor who was employed in their works, to exploit it commercially under patent, with copper, gold and silver. This upset most of the silver platers in London, Sheffield and Birmingham, and also challenged the tinplate and japanning trades. Correspondence between the Elkingtons and a Benjamin Smith mentions a proposed partnership with John Wright, but the Elkingtons withdrew from this, although later, during their partnership with Mason were committed to paying Wright an annuity.

It was considered by many of Mason's friends to be a risky business for him to enter, but he obviously realised its potential. It also met his desire only to embark on an enterprise when, "two things are connected with it: a great difficulty to be overcome, or a large amount of capital to be laid out". On the 29 March, 1842 he entered into a formal partnership with the Elkingtons and they began to trade as Elkington, Mason and Co. in Newhall Street, (21) and for some reason on the 27 April, 1849 a fresh partnership deed was drawn up. R.E. Leader, who established the Elkington Archive, comments that, "Mr. Elkington put £55,000 into the business contrary to Bunce, Mason's contribution was £35,000 reduced to £27,500, and profits were one third to Mason and two thirds to G.R. Elkington". (22) (23)

At first the pioneers were looked upon as wild impractical men. However, in 1849 the grounds of Bingley House in Broad Street became the temporary home of "An Exhibition of the Manufactures of Birmingham and the Midland Counties". This early showcase of design and industrial art was visited by Prince Albert, and was probably taken up as an idea for the Great Exhibition of 1851, and from then on the partners became influential directors of an expanding industry, and collectors of works of art.

Much of the technical success of this work was attributable to Alexander Parkes, an able chemist and inventor. He was so closely connected with the process, that on one occasion, when giving evidence in court he was described as "the Nestor of electro-metall-urgy". Among his patents was one gained in 1843, for the electro-plating of flowers and fragile natural objects, and when Prince Albert visited the Elkington and Mason works in Birmingham, he was presented with an example of Parkes's works, a spiders web which had been coated in silver.

The partners built a factory with workshops and a showroom on what is now the site of the Birmingham Science Museum in Newhall Street, to produce and display electroplated "articles of taste". These included vases and sculptures, and involved the work of artists as well as craftsmen. The importance that Elkington and Mason attached to applied art was shown by the fact that 50 or 60 of their assistants attended the classes in design at the Midland Institute.

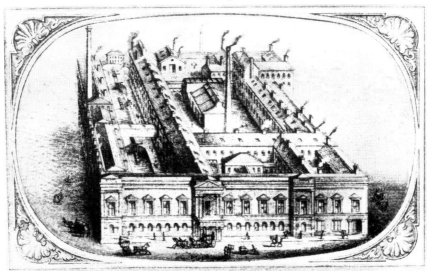

21. *Elkington, Mason & Co., Electro-Plating Works, Newhall Street.*

22. G.R. Elkington.

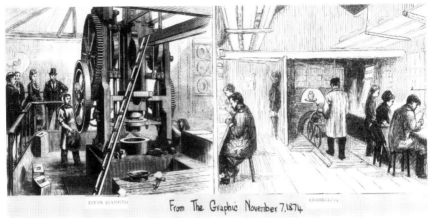

STEAM STAMPING

From The Graphic November 7,1874

ENAMELLING

23. Part of the electro-plating process at Elkington, Mason & Co.

There was some speculation at the time as to who had provided the thousands of pounds for the Newhall Street building. Leader quoting from G.R. Elkington's diary stated that, building work began on 20 May, 1838, and that the building was opened on 28 November, 1838, and that Bunce's comments were incorrect, in implying that Mason drew up the plans. He says that there was no association between Mason and the Elkingtons before 1840, and that these must all be references to extension plans. There is no doubting Leader's enthuiasm to debunk Bunce, for he also takes issue with the reference, that the Brearley Street works were attributable to Mason, and states that they were in the possession of the firm before Mason joined. He indicates that Krupp's work in developing his fork and spoon invention, and the abortive India rubber ring experiments had been carried out there.

Mason was sceptical about available markets for the rather expensive "articles of taste" - vases and the like - he thought that the future depended on producing small cheap everyday articles. Things which were within the means of the masses, like jewellery and cutlery. So when the next factory was opened in Brearley Street it produced elecrtoplated spoons and forks which became very popular and boosted trade considerably.

There is some confusion as to whether Mason visited Germany to study new techniques, but what did take place was the visit of Alfred Krupp from Essen, Germany with an introduction from Siemen to try and interest Mason and Elkington in his invention - a machine for rolling metal blanks for spoons and forks. He offered it to the partners, for what Mason considered an exorbitant price, so he was offered £10,000 and told to go away and think about it. The offer was accepted, and the machine installed at the Brearley Street works. According to Mason, Krupp offered him a partnership, which he declined, but the £10,000 helped establish the great Krupps steel-works at Essen. It is interesting to speculate how different decisions on these matters might have changed world history, as these works were so crucial to the Germans in the production of armaments during the First and Second World Wars.

Birmingham soon became the centre of the electroplating trade, with expanding markets in this country, Europe and America, and to cope with demand large warehouses and showrooms were opened in Liverpool and London. The popularity of the goods was shown by the large number of exhibits at the Great Exhibition of 1851, which included the Great Exhibition Sheild (24) designed for Elkington and Mason by Luke Limmer - the pseudonym adopted by the illustrator John Leighton.

24. Commemoration Shield designed for the Great Exhibition 1851, Elkington, Mason & Co.

A visit to the electroplating works is recorded in the Ironmonger of 31 October, 1864 as follows, "It is entirely to Messrs. Elkington, Mason & Co. of Newhall Street, Birmingham, that the introduction of elecrtoplated articles is due. The company carry on three distinct manufactures at their extensive works in Newhall Street: the reproduction and manufacture of works of art in copper, silver and gold; ordinary silversmiths' work; and the making and electroplating of articles of ordinary domestic use, such as tea-pots, forks, spoons, knives, etc. It is only with the latter we have anything to do, although the numerous electro-bronze specimens shown to us might well occupy a place in the shops of most of our readers". (25)

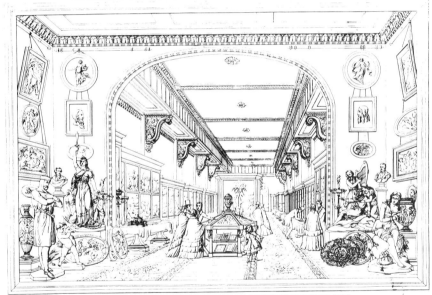

25. Elkington, Mason & Co., showrooms Birmingham.

The partnership was also involved, although to a lesser extent in the India rubber ring trade. They were manufactured under the patents of Macintosh and others, processes which rendered the materials tough and elastic by impregnating them with sulphur under heat. However, Alexander Parkes, who worked closely with Mason devised, in 1841, a process - which he sold to the partners for £5,000 - whereby fabrics could be waterproofed by being immersed in a cold solution of India rubber in bisulphide of carbon, to achieve the same result without the unpleasant sulphur smell. Despite the fact that it was successfully carried out by Elkington and Mason at Brearly Street, Birmingham for several years, difficulties arose over the patents, and they were sold in 1852 to the original manufacturers Macintosh and Co. of Manchester, for an estimated £80,000. It was by then extensively used and known all over the world as, "the cold converting process".

An enlightened aspect of the partnership was their offer, in January 1853, of prizes to workmen in their employ for suggestions to improve processes within their extensive business enterprise. There were also in addition to the usual apprenticeship indentures, written agreements drawn up with workmen involved in coating and metallurgy.

On the 31 July, 1852, Henry Elkington retired and so the partnership was dissolved, but he survived only a few months dying on 26 October, 1852. But a new agreement was drawn up with George Richard Elkington which lasted for 14 years until his death on the 22 September, 1865, at the age of 63. Mason related how he experienced a strange feeling at the time. Aware that Elkington was very ill and possibly dying at his home Pool Park, near Ruthin, Denbighshire he heard music coming from the chimney and was immediately aware of the death. He related this to his wife, Annie, before they received the news, and was so moved by the experience that he was often heard recalling the event.

A Government Report in 1864 gave the following account of the Elkington, Mason & Co. electroplating enterprise: "The articles are firstly cut out from flat bars of metal by powerful steam machinery, in shape so as to leave very little scrap or waste metal. These rough pieces are afterwards put through rollers and stamps till they gradually take roughly the shape required. The spoons and forks rolling machinery is attended by a foreman and 16 or 17 young women, one to put into each machine and one to take out. These, it is said, are generally, though perhapes not always, over 18.... The fly-wheel is also securely fenced, as well as the machinery and bands in other parts of the works. They would otherwise be sources of great danger, especially to women....

After the articles have been thus roughly formed, they need filing out, smoothing and preparing to receive the electro-plate, when on, is finished......In the finishing processes powders are used, as prepared lime and oil for the buffing, and in the colouring. These, especially where a bobbin or mop is used, cause a great deal of dust, which settles plentifully on the heads and dresses of the workpeople and other places... Mr. George Ireland, Manager.. I do not think that they ought to go to work of any kind, under the age of twelve, and should be glad of a law to enforce this........ A pity that females should work in factories at all as it interferes with their proper life, domestic. It is bad for girls under 14 to work in a factory, with elder females, as there are sure to be at least two whose conversation is not fit for them to hear. I take all the pains that I can to ensure proper behaviour, by ascertaining, as far as I am able, the previous character, and discharging in cases of immorality, as if an unmarried women gives birth to a child.... I consider that Sunday Schools have great influence for good, and that persons who attend them are likely to be more respectful and orderly than those who do not, and accordingly in my inquiries I take such attendance as one test of character. This is a poor and very indifferent neighbourhood, and I should think it probable that the greater part in it do not attend Sunday School.

There is every facility for education in Birmingham, most of the Sunday Schools, dissenting as well as Church, having week-day schools attached to them. But there is also great demand for young labour, - greater I should say than for adults -, that children are taken from school by there parents, as soon as any employment can be got for them, and this in some kinds of work, is very early indeed, as young as 6. I should also be very glad of a law limiting the hours of labour of young people in all employments to a reasonable amount. The hours in this establishment are already within the factory limit, and scarcely vary. It is true that the articles made here are of the plain kind, as forks, spoons, and small miscellaneious solid-ware articles, as snuffers & c... The ornamental articles are made in the Newhall Street department".

From 1865 the business was wholly carried out by Elkington's sons, and Mason had no further involvement, concentrating all his efforts on the Lancaster Street pen factory. In accordance with the Companies Act 1862, a Memorandum of Association shows that on 18 May, 1887, Elkington & Co. became an incorporated company. In 1907 the company was dissolved and became a limited company. After the Second World War Elkington & Co. was taken over by the Delta Metal Company of East Greenwich and Birmingham, and the firm moved to Walsall.

In parallel with the electroplating business the partners secured a patent from the firms chemist, Alexander Parkes - for which he was paid in lieu of obtaining a licence - for melting copper ores and purifying the copper with phosphorous, but the process required a smelting works. So in 1850 Mason visited South Wales to look for a possible site. He first visited Swansea, but moved on because of his wish that his workforce should enjoy as much fresh air as possible. He or they, as the Elkington's were very involved in this project, eventually purchased 20 acres of cheap derelict land near Pembrey, at the mouth of the River Burry three miles from Llanelli. This was a suitable and convenient situation for receiving and smelting Cornish ore. The Works (26a) built, was described as "excellent works laid out, large well built and specially designed to secure the health of the men engaged in them". Houses with gardens were built around the works, and with the original village of Towyn Bach this eventually became Pembrey, and later Burry Port. In addition to the Copperworks Mason and Elkington owned and leased several collieries, and owned three brickworks.

26a *Remains of Mason & Elkington's Copper Works, Pembrey, South Wales, built around 1850 - aerial view about 1935.*

Mason took an interest in the education and religious instruction of the children and using bricks from the brickworks, built in 1855, at a cost of £1,700 separate boys, girls and infant schools (26b) which together accommodated 500 pupils from the village. They were opened by Mason on the 22 August, 1855. In line with Mason's views the schools were non-denominational, an exception to all the other schools in the parish controlled by the Established Church, a decision which pleased the local Non-conformists.

26b Copperworks School built 1855.

The local smelters and colliers were suspicious of his motives, and did not want their children to learn English. So to encourage attendance he provided hats, bonnets, shoes and clothing of all kinds. When they began to attend on a regular basis, he charged the parents one penny (½p) a week.

The partnership between Mason and G.R. Elkington trading as copper smelters in Pembrey and Birmingham was dissolved as Mason wished to retire, and Elkington agreed to continue the business under the old name. Eventually the main interest in the company at Pembrey was acquired by Elliot's Metal Company Limited.

Mason as usual had other irons in the fire, and had turned his attention to nickel plating. Charles Adkin's discovery of how to refine crude nickel ore, in 1832, turned into the basis of an industry. Nickel plating became a very common way of protecting metal parts from corrosion and rust, in an attractive way. It was, therefore, extensively used not only in the jewellery and silverplate trades as a cheap substitute for silver, but in the hollow-ware, cutlery, weighing machine, button, pin, cycle and lamp trades. The new demand for nickel and cobalt engendered a search for new methods of refining and new sources of the ore.

Mason and Alexander Parkes set up a Nickel Refining factory in the 1850's, known as the Brace or Constructors, after Samuel Carpenter's brace and small steam engine factory which was operating on the site in 1833. It stood by the canal at the lower end of Holly Lane, Erdington. The canal bridge, although since rebuilt, still bears the name Brace Factory Bridge. An old building which could still be identified in 1988, as part of the Constructors Works at the side of the canal at Holly Lane, was reputed to be part of this, the first nickel manufacturing works in the world. The business lost heavily for several years, but they persevered and eventually became successful.

The company referred to as Mason, Hayes and Co. nickel and cobalt ore refiners, Birches Green Nickel Works, Erdington, registered as a Limited Company, November 17, 1876 was Mason's company. There were also a number of references in the Ironmonger which refer to this company, including an item on June 18, 1881, about Mason importing New Caledonian ores never before refined, and of his being the largest nickel maker in the world, to the point where his process cut nickel prices from 11/- to 2/6 a pound. This was the one industry which Mason built up, and with which he still had contact at the time of his death, and which he left in his Will to his nephew Martyn J. Smith. There is a later reference to the nickel refinery being sold by Mason's nephew, Martyn J. Smith, to the Nickel Co. Ltd., Paris, of which Smith was a director, and then a further article on the 25 March, 1882, indicating that the Nickel Co. Ltd., Erdington was fully employed. But on February 24, 1894, the Nickel Company moved to London.

Chapter 7
Orphanage

When Mason began to contemplate philanthropy in the 1850's, the main focus of his attention was to provide for women and children in need - men were thought capable of looking after themselves. One account states that a frequent participant to these discussions was Alexander Parkes, the chemist, who often stayed with the Mason's. Parkes made the suggestion of an orphanage at Erdington, during an evening when Annie Mason had mooted the disposal of her husbands income and mentioned it to him when he came in, he suggested that she go to bed, while he and Parkes talk it over. They sat up until after 11 o'clock, discussing and elaborating the proposal. Parkes was surprised that Mason had stayed up so late. However, the result was effective, for in less than a fortnight with the assistance of Isaac Newey of Erdington, drew up plans for almshouses for 30 women and a home for 20 or 30 orphans. Whether on this, as according to Willert Beale, he was inclined to do on all other important issues, he consulted Isaac Horton, a pork butcher in the Bull Ring, Birmingham is not known. Although in this instance Beale's sarcasm was somewhat misplaced. Horton was no ordinary butcher but among other things a very wealthy landowner, and property speculator, who purchased large blocks of buildings, many in the best locations in the town centre. He assisted Mason with his philanthropic enterprises and was often involved in the land purchase transactions.

However with or without advice the first orphanage was to provide thirty almshouses for spinsters and widows, aged fifty or over, and the remainder for orphan girls, but because of the great demand the plans had to be enlarged to accommodate 50 girls. The building was started in 1855 and opened in 1858, in Sheep Street, Erdington - later renamed Station Road. This large building was of Gothic design with two gabled wings and a central tower. At the front was a low wall with an arched entrance gateway. The entrance hall had an open timbered roof and a large window over the doorway. There were 20 sets of rooms. (27)

27. *First alms houses and orphanage built by Mason, Station Road, Erdington, 1858.*

Mason gave preference to Birmingham and Kidderminster children, in order to give them opportunities he had been denied. One of the first residents was Mrs Bakewell, widow of Bakewell, who purchased the business of Richard Griffiths, Mason's father-in-law, which caused him so much distress.

The use of this building was changed - when the new orphanage was built in 1869 - to accommodate 31 women in almshouses. The accommodation provided the women with a furnished home in rooms 14 feet by 11 feet by 9 feet, with coal and gas provided, and a small annual income. Later a sitting room, kitchen, storerooms and a dormitory were used to meet the needs of 18 girls who had been educated at the main orphanage, but were either too sick or could not obtain work in service. Then in the early 1880's the whole building was converted into homes for 26 elderly women. It was demolished, apart from the boundary wall along Station Road in 1974 and the land used to build a nursery school.

Almost as soon as the first building was completed Mason felt dissatisfied and was determined to build something on a more extensive scale. His first concern was to obtain the support of people from across the religious denominations. He decided to approach Dr. J.C. Miller the Rector of St. Martins, who at first seemed little interested in the idea. Miller was unaware of Mason's wealth and commitment, and had no knowledge of Mason himself - which tends to confirm the fact that Mason was little known outside the business community. However, a greater rapport was established when Mason mentioned that he was willing to commit £100,000 to the project. It was then agreed that a meeting of interested people would be called, and shortly afterwards twenty of them, including ministers and clergymen met at Miller's house. In all, ten or twelve meetings were held, but there were fundamental differences of opinion, particularly over Mason's wish that scripture be taught, but his objection to the teaching of the catechism, and as to whether children from the respectable class or those from the "gutter" were to be offered help. Then in 1857 Mason wrote the following letter which seemed to encapsulate his thoughts and feelings.

Norwood House,
Erdington,
22 May 1857

My Dear Sir,

Let me heartily thank you and Mr. Lea and other friends for the kind attention you have given to my request for your advice and assistance in reference to the foundation and opening of the proposed Orphanage, and let me beg of you to assure all the friends who have kindly interested themselves in the matter how greatly I feel obliged.

I deeply regret that Mr. Lea and yourself do not feel at liberty to give that unreserved and cordial support to the Institution which you would have done but for the objection I have to the introduction of the Church of England Catechism, as a basis for the religious instruction of the children.

My views on this matter have been formed for many years. I confess when I first made my appeal to you for help, I was not without fear that I should encounter difficulty on this account and I cannot tell you how happy I felt after our first interview from the impression I received upon my mind (from our conversation at that time) that you would be both willing and able to act in perfect union with brethren of all other denominations holding the same doctrinal views as yourself.

I trust however for the sake of the class of poor peoples children whose welfare I have at heart that the Institution will still receive the friendly aid of yourself and of all our Church of England friends, not withstanding the supposed mistaken view of the Founder which has unhappily occasioned the interference with his original design for the foundation.

I have given my best attention to the earnest advice you gave to me on Tuesday last in such a kind and Christian spirit, but my opinion remains unchanged.

I dare not in fixing the terms of the foundation which will I trust govern the institution for future years permit the introduction (so far as I am able to prevent it) of that mode of imparting religious instruction which to my mind would be erroneous and dangerous to the poor children the walfare of whose souls as well as bodies I would fane promote, in the way which commands itself to my judgement, as the only way which God himself has instructed us to follow.

I believe the Holy Scriptures to contain the only safe instruction, which under the teaching of God's spirit, are able now as formerly when "known from a child to make wise unto salvation through faith which is in Christ Jesus".

As Mr. Lea declines to act as a Trustee or Committeeman, and as you cannot act with entire cordiality, and as other Church of England friends, may probably feel the same kind of difficulty, it would certainly deprive me and I think other friends of much of the pleasure and satisfaction we should have derived from a hearty working in such a labour of love, with good men of all shades of opinion in minor matters and so I fear the Institution would suffer loss... I think it best under the altered circumstances to appoint a body of lay men only as Trustees.

I shall still feel it a duty to exclude all Catechisms, and to direct that the religious instruction to be given to the children shall be only scriptural, and leave to the care of the committee the mode of giving it.

I think too that from what has transpired it will not be wise to make it imperative to the Trust Deed, that a chaplain should be appointed, but leave this also to the Committee.

I have endeavoured to make myself clearly understood in order to save trouble to you and your friends, and whilst I do very much regret, that we do not see eye to eye in this matter, I am not without hope that the Institution will still enjoy the sympathy of yourself and friends; and under any and every circumstance that it will be commenced and hereafter conducted in such a trustful and dependent spirit, that the blessing of God may rest upon it, and that he will put into the hearts of many a desire to sustain and carry it on

for the promotion of his glory in the present and eternal good of the poor helpless children, who may from time to time be brought under its protection and influence.
Again sincerely thanking you.

I remain sir
Yours faithfully J.M.

The Rev. J.C. Miller D.D.
St. Martin's Rectory, Birmingham.

The Mr. Lea referred to in this letter was the Rev. G. Lea, vicar of St. George's Church, Edgbaston, for 18 years.

Mason felt that he was more interested in meeting the needs of poor orphans, than many of those he had consulted, so decided to undertake the project alone. The site he chose was adjacent to Norwood House, his home in Erdington. With his usual determination he appointed J.R. Botham, a Birmingham architect, to draw up plans, and the foundation stone was laid by Mason, privately, on the 19 September, 1860, and the work began in 1865. According to reports the project drew little attention until the towers began to dominate the skyline. In true Victorian tradition the building was to be strong, large, ornamental and built to last. (28)

It was completed and handed over to the Trustees on the 29 July, 1869. Amazingly the opening ceremony was performed by six gentlemen meeting at Mason's house. Valued at £60,000 and endowed to the value of £200,000 it stood majestically with its frontage to Bell Lane. The accommodation was for 26 women and 300 children, on a thirteen acre site with playgrounds, gardens, woods and fields. Prominently situated on open ground; the 200 foot centre tower was visible for miles around. Built in true Lomardic style as an irregular oblong 207 feet on the North West entrance front to Bell Lane, 190 feet to the North East playground front, 300 feet to the East garden side and 270 feet to the West side where the out offices were placed. It was three storeys high with rows of semi-circular leaded rose windows with buttresses, and carved mouldings. The gabled ends of the building projected slightly and were mounted with coloured figures of angels with folded wings.

Dormer windows let light into the dormitories. The whole structure was dominated by the three towers, one 200 feet contained a clock with a 25 hundredweight court bell which struck the hours, with Cambridge chimes on 4 bells, this cost £600, another tower 120 feet high at the entrance and the third 110 feet, which aided ventilation, and served as a chimney for all the flues of the building. There was a hot water central heating system, which also provided steam used for cooking, washing and drying. Mason took a particulat interest in these feats of engineering.

28. Second and main orphanage built by Mason, Bell Lane, Erdington, 1868.

It is interesting that the archtect J.R. Botham, at an early stage, because of what were stated to be private reasons, gave up supervising the construction of the building, which was then taken over by Mason.

Other impressive aspects were the fact that it was built with three million bricks made on the orphanage land. Hell stone was used for the basement with Derbyshire and Shrewsbury stone for the mouldings, strong corners, buttresses and windows.

The inside was simply designed but on a large scale with large dining rooms, numerous corridors and staircases. (29) The main dining room was 70 feet by 30 feet, with massive tables and chairs, this led into other large rooms for sewing, music and drill. An

29. Orphanage, Bell Lane, Erdington, principal staircase.

orphaned child from small overcrowded accommodation must have been somewhat overawed by such a place. Yet, for its time, it was seen as a magnificent modern establishment with up-to-date equipment, which included such modern facilities as water closets. Although it appears that when they became offensive, they were replaced by dry closets, the contents of which were deposited in a large vault next to the engine room. No doubt this was an example of Mason's ingenuity, as the ashes were used as a deodoriser.

Mason was very keen to ensure the future management and finance of the orphanage, so the drawing up of the Trust Deed of Foundation of the Orphanage and Almshouses on 29 July, 1868, was of great concern to him. This task was given to his solicitor and friend Palmer, but he unfortunately died and the matter had to be referred to G.J. Johnson of Tyndall, Johnson and Tyndall. Under the Mortmain Act the Trust Deed to be effective had to be in existence for 12 months of the founders life, and concern that Mason might die during this period, prompted his solicitors to draw up a deed transferring all the estates of the Orphanage endowment to a wealthy aquaintance Robert Lucas Chance, a prominent Birmingham citizen. This was a device for ensuring that the endowments were secure for the qualifying twelve months period, which ended 31 July, 1869. On that day Mason formerly presided over a meeting of the Trustees and declared the Orphanage officially open.

To safeguard the future of the Orphanage and its non-sectarian foundation, Mason arranged that control should pass to the Town Council after his death. At a meeting of the Town Council on August 3, the Mayor read the following letter from Josiah Mason:-

Norwood House,
Erdington,
August 2nd, 1869

Dear Mr. Mayor,

I herewith send you a printed copy of the foundation deed of the Orphanage and Almshouses which I have lately built there, and endowed with upwards of a thousand acres of freehold land, in the neighbourhood of Birmingham, besides land and buildings in Birmingham itself. This deed of endowment, although made more than twelve months ago, is, as you may be aware, not legally complete until twelve months after its execution. That period having now elapsed, it is proper I should make this communication to you officially, for the following reason:- One of the most serious difficulties I had in settling the endowment scheme was how to provide against the administration of the charity falling under the exclusive control of any religious sect or party, or the funds being diverted from their proper purpose. After much consideration I have conducted that the most effectual means of accomplishing my object was to place my trust under the superintendence of my fellow-townmen, acting, through their municipal representatives, in such a mode that whilst it should really place in their hands the means of securing the efficient administration of property, which is already considerable, and which, from its nature, must increase with the prosperity of Birmingham. During my own life, or so long as I have health and strength, I trust to be able, with the assistance of the seven gentlemen I have named trustees, to continue the administration of the charity.

Immediately after my death, if the Town Council will do me the honour to render the slight assistance I ask in the promotion of my scheme, they will have to elect an equal number of trustees to those I have named, making the number fourteen, viz., seven private and seven official trustees. The seven official trustees may be either members of the Council, or not, as the Council for the time being may determine. Whenever any vacancy shall happen in the number of official trustees, nominated by the Council, the Council will fill up such vacancy. Whenever any vacancy happened in the number of private trustees, the whole body of trustees (in which the Town Council will always have the advantage of seven votes to six) will fill up that vacancy. The only restriction I have imposed on the trustees is that they shall be Protestant laymen, resident within ten miles of the Orphanage. In order also that the Town Council may have more frequent opportunities of supervising the finances of the trust than would be afforded by the appointment of trustees (which after the first appointment would be infrequent), I have provided that the accounts of the charity shall be audited by a public accountant once a year, and that a copy of such accounts shall be transmitted to the Town Clerk of the borough. By these means I trust that my charity may always have the advantage of a small executive body elected by, and therefore commanding the respect of their fellow-townsmen, and preserved from all improper influences, by being placed under the control of the public opinion of the town. It will be a great satisfaction to me to know that the Town Council of the borough of Birmingham will be willing to accept the trust I have reposed in them, and for that purpose I shall be glad if you bring the matter before them in due course.

I am, dear Mr. Mayor,

Yours truly,
JOSIAH MASON

Henry Holland, Esq.,
Mayor of Birmingham.

The letter was referred to the General Purposes Committee, with instruction to report their opinion as to the mode in which the Council, on behalf of the borough, might best testify their high appreciation of Mason's noble charity. It was accepted to be acted upon following Mason's death.

Following Mason's death G.J. Johnson, Solicitor, on behalf of the Trustees, wrote in July 1881, from 36, Waterloo Street, Birmingham to the Mayor Richard Chamberlain, informing him of the Council's power to appoint seven Trustees for the Orphanage, who had to be laymen, Protestants and living within 10 miles of the Orphanage, but not necesssarily members of the Council. This information appears in the Council Minutes, 5 July, 1881.

The Trust Deed was an extensive document of 63 pages, dated, 29 July, 1868. It contained the endowments of the Orphanage which consisted of about 1,032 acres of freehold land, about 200 acres of valuable building land in Erdington, including Norwood House, Bell Lane (later renamed Orphanage Road), (30) Mason's own property, with groves and gardens totalling 13 acres, and the rest in the parishes of Northfield, Bickenhill, Feckenham, Sutton Coldfield and other places in Warwickshire and Worcestershire. About two and a half acres consisted of land and buildings in the centre of Birmingham. One twenty year old property alone had a rental of more than £1,500 a year, and the total rental value of the Orphanage estates was around £10,000 a year, with a capital value of £209,000. Most of this property which Mason bought at around £120 an acre, had by 1881 increased in value to £500 an acre.

The Deed also outlined the qualifications for admission, children had to be under 9 years of age, the legitimate child of both parents now dead, and before admission, certificates of birth, marriage of parents and their death certificates had to be presented. They could be admitted from anywhere in the country or abroad, with special consideration given to children from Kidderminster and Birmingham. Boys normally remained until the age 12 or 14, and girls 16 or 18, and on leaving were given two complete sets of clothes, but some remained longer in the service of the orphanage in order to become teachers or assistants. During their stay they were trained to refrain from alcohol, and join the Band of Hope. Trustees

30. *Map of Erdington and surrounding area 1881.*

could dismiss children for disobedience, misconduct or other reasonable cause or return them to relatives or friends who may be able to provide. Their friends and relatives were only allowed to visit twice a year, although other visits could be arranged if they obtained written permission. (31)

Children were to be lodged, clothed, fed, maintained and educated. They were to be taught reading, writing, spelling, English grammar, arithmetic, geography, history and holy scripture. In addition girls were to be taught sewing, baking, cooking, washing, mangling and all ordinary household and domestic duties, with shoe repairing for the boys - no equality of opportunity here. The children were under the supervision of the Matron, Miss Stockwin, the sub- Matron, her sister Ann Stockwin, a schoolmaster, drillmaster, sewing mistress and outdoor mistress. Great emphasis was placed on physical training and upon the industrial education of the boys, and the domestic skills of the girls - who were expected to do all the housework. Mason was caught up in the movement for universal compulsory education, and wished to place his school under government inspection, but much to his disappointment as a boarding school they were excluded.

Sir Josiah Mason's Orphanage.

ORDINARY VISITATION DAYS.

RULES FOR VISITORS.

Children's surnames beginning with the following letters, **A, B C, D, E, F** can be seen on the *Tuesday*. Those beginning with **G, H, I, J, K, L, M, N, O, P** to be seen on the *Wednesday*, and those beginning with **Q, R, S, T, U, V, W, X, Y**, and **Z** may be seen on the *Thursday*.

Each Orphan may be visited by three persons only, in one party, between the hours of 3 and 5 o'clock in the afternoon, on the following days.

IN JANUARY.—The first Tuesday, Wednesday, and Thursday *in the one week.*

IN JUNE.—The last Tuesday, Wednesday, and Thursday *in the one week.*

A SPECIAL ORDER must be obtained for admission at any other time by observing these three directions :—

1.—Write to the Secretary, Sir Josiah Mason's Orphanage, Erdington, Birmingham.

2.—State the grounds of your application, and—

3.—Enclose a stamped envelope with your name and address for answer.

DIRECTIONS AS TO GIFTS.

For the sake of the health and discipline of the Orphans, it is desirable that presents should not be made of any articles of food except oranges, nuts, apples, and ripe fruit.

The following are allowed :—Balls, bats, tops, books, hoops, marbles, magnifying glasses, scissors, needles, pins, skipping ropes, thimbles, dolls, workboxes, toys of a useful kind, &c.

31. Sir Josiah Mason's Orphanage rules for visitors.

The childrens health care was undertaken by two homeopathic doctors, Dr. Gibbs Blake and Mr. Wynne Thomas. They were encouraged in this by Mason, who was a disciple of Hahemann, the founder of modern homeopathic treatment. The children it appears had very little choice in the matter of their medical treatment.

The demand for places increased, so that in 1874 an additional wing had to be built, it consisted of dormitories, and a school room for 150 boys. This was connected to the main building by a large dining hall, capable of accommodating 500 children. The orphanage was then capable of accommodating 300 girls, 150 boys and 50 infant boys, who all met together for meals and prayers but were separated for school and dormitory. Between 1869 and 1881 406 girls were admitted to the orphanage, 29 of whom, according to the register died, 175 were sent to service or returned to friends, of the 246 boys admitted, 7 died, 114 went into employment or returned to friends.

The children's religious needs were not neglected, and despite Mason's non-sectarian views, religious services were, in the main, conducted by Wesleyan Methodist Ministers. Local people were encouraged to attend the chapel, and could sit in the gallery, which held 200.

In accordance with Mason's wishes, trustees had to be laymen and Protestants residing within 10 miles of the orphanage. The seven original trustees were Frederick Allen, jeweller; William Bach, miner; William Fothergill Batho, engineer; James Gibbs Blake, doctor; Isaac North, provision merchant; Thomas Shaw, bank manager, all of Birmingham and John Christopher Yeomans of Erdington gentlemen. With Mason as founder they constituted the first Board of Management. They were Wesleyans, Congregationalists, Baptists, Unitarians and members of the Society of Friends, and so no doubt complied with Mason's religious intentions. One of the later trustees was Solomon Jevons. He was a Wesleyan Methodist and one of the founders of the Princess Alice Orphanace, at New Oscott, based it was said on ideas obtained in discussion with his friend Mason. They were near neighbours in Erdington and a close friendship sprang up between them. Jevons was a lay reader at the first orphanage.

After Mason's death, trustees were never to be less than 10, and not more than 14, of whom 7 were always to be nominated by the Town Council of Birmingham, and must be laymen or Protestants. Finally the deed said that during the life of the founder, applications may be made for a Royal Charter or a special Act of Parliament incorporating the trust under the name of Josiah Mason Orphanage and Almshouses Trust.

Mason was very proud of his achievement and visited the orphanage regularly. It was said that on Sundays he would stand at the head of the long centre table in the dining room to preside over the mid-day meal. Then on occasions when he entered the grounds the children flocked around him, calling him daddy or father. One can imagine how much this all meant to this benevolent paternalistic figure.

One of the most famous or notorious residents was Horatio William Bottomley, who was placed at age 11 by the Duke of Argyll, through Holyoake. He became a journalist of some repute as editor of the Financial Times from 1898-1900. Involved himself, with Mr. Vernon a solicitor, in the trial of Dr. Crippen the infamous muderer and influenced the famous advocate Marshall Hall so that he did not defend Crippen. He also created and was editor of John Bull. From 1906-1912 he was M.P. for South Hackney and was elected again in 1918. However, he was constantly in court. In 1922 he received a 7 year prison sentence for his John Bull scheme to attract investment in government bonds, which was exposed as a fraud to divert money to his own use.

Although the orphanage name remained as a legal entity, for administrative purposes it was designated a school, and in accordance with the recommendations of the Curtis Report the term orphanage was dropped. Later the school was opened to day pupils under Birmingham Education Department. Reunions are still held each year on the last Saturday in June in the grounds of the Trust at Olton.

During the Second World War cottages were built on land next to the orphanage in Bell Lane (Orphanage Road). Some of the residents of the Sheep Street (Station Road) almshouses were moved there, together with the residents of Dowell's Retreat, Bordesley whose buildings had been damaged by a bomb. They remained there until December 1951 when maisonettes 1-33 were added to Dowell's Retreat and it was renamed Mason House. The cottages survived the demolition of the orphanage in 1963 and are still in use today.

In the 1960's it became evident that the building was outdated. The heating and general upkeep became very expensive. The trustees took the decision to demolish the building (32) and sell the land. The site was sold by auction, at Regent House, St. Philip's Place, Colmore Row, by H. Donald Dixon & Co., on the 10 January, 1964, at 2.30pm. It comprised 6.15 acres with a frontage of 517 feet and the land was sold with outline planning permission and vacant possession. An estate of houses and Yenton School now occupy the site.

The sale raised £106,000 which was used by the Sir Josiah Mason Trust to build accommodation for older people at Mason Court, Olton.

32. Demolition of the Orphanage.

Chapter 8
Orphan's Reminiscences

Former residents have left an interesting record of their time at the orphanage. Their reminiscences were put together at the request of the trustees in 1931, and completed in 1933. These graphic accounts of life in a 19th Century institution show some of the worst excesses of child care in those far off days, but also highlight individual acts of kindness.

Many of them vividly recalled been taken by relatives to see Mason at his Lancaster Street office, or at the orphanage, meeting the awesome founder with his flowing white hair and beard, and awaiting their fate. A boy admitted from Somerset on the 3 January 1872, was received by the Matron Miss Stockwin and was shocked by the appearance of the other boys. Three or four of the younger ones wore frocks of tartan plaid, which according to this account, allowed them to be chastised more easily. All the rest wore long heavy corduroy trousers, "Blucher", Prussian style boots with "gutta-percha" rubberised soles, grey jacket with a hook at the top, but no buttons, and round calico caps. The uniform gave them a rough and untidy appearance. When boys moved on to their first pair of long trousers they paraded before Mason and received money. They were also allocated numbers, and must have felt the heavy pressure and depersonalisation of institution life. The girl's wore uniforms of white pinafore and brown frock. Belts were worn for best, which had white metal buckles with the motto "Do Deeds of Love" engraved on them. The badge and buttons worn included the mermaid and the words "God is Love, Do Deed of Love". In the main, the children thought the clothes very plain, and the design on the button silly, but felt it a great punishment to have the belts and buckles taken off them for misbehaviour.

Many recalled the reasons for, and the actual circumstances of their admission. Some recalled the early 1870's when there was an outbreak of smallpox, which meant many children lost both parents within a matter of days. One recollection of such an event involved a whole family who had contracted smallpox, the parents died, but the three boys survived - although they had pitted faces. Relatives said "We cannot have them, send them to the workhouse". They were all eventually admitted to the orphanage.

Another family of four from Rugby suffered a similar fate following smallpox in 1874. Their father, an engine driver was thought to have brought it from Manchester - although it was already in the neighbourhood. Relatives left food on the doorstep and threw stones at the window to attract their attention. When their parents died Miss Nicholson, the lady of the manor, took them in. She knew of Mason's work and arranged interviews for three of the children. One of them described the scene of arriving at the orphanage, accompanied by this rather old fashioned lady. She rang the bell which echoed through the long corridor. Then the great door was opened and they were ushered into the waiting room. Later they were interviewed by Mason, but only two of them were accepted for admission. One of the boys, Alfred Henry, had weak eyes and his admission was delayed until they improved. He returned in 1875 and was then admitted.

In another recorded incident, two small boys aged 7 and 8 sat on the bank opposite the orphanage on a fine summer afternoon with their grandmother. Early for their appointment, and overawed by the building (33) they waited until the clock struck 4p.m., before ringing the bell. They were received by Miss Stockwin and Matthews, the secretary, and within a few minutes they were saying tearful goodbyes to their grandmother, and had become "inmates" of the orphanage.

On some days there were several admissions, with many of the children in tears and in need of consolation. In one particular instance, there was a grandfather who knew something of Mason. He visited accompanied by his grandson, who wished to see his brother and sister in the orphanage, Mason said "Mary's not very well, why not change her for her brother". The exchange was arranged and took place three weeks later, but there is no record of the feelings of the children concerned, or their relatives, to this rather unusual arrangement.

According to those who saw Mason on his visits to the orphanage, he was always dressed in black with a double Inverness cape and round felt hat, and could have been taken for a non-conformist minister. It was perhaps this leaning towards things plain which aroused the complaints about the clothing which easily identified the wearer as a member of an institution. It may also have influenced the design of the dining room and boys house in 1874, which was thought monstrous by the children, and nicknamed the cowshed, because of its bare and whitewashed interior.

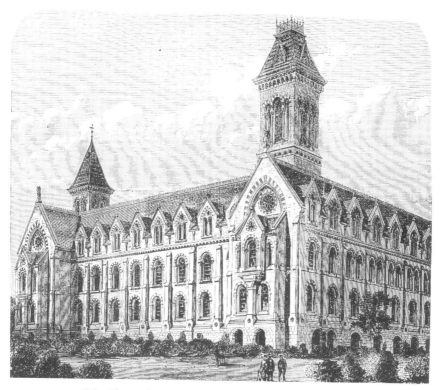

33. Sir Josiah Mason's Orphanage, Erdington.

Some remember Mason's kindly reassuring smile and fatherly pat on the head, and thought him unaware of the brutality of some of the staff. Particular mention was made of Mr. & Mrs. Dillon who appear very sadistic. They used the lavatory as a place of punishment, gaining for it the reputation of a torture chamber. Some recall being beaten black and blue by the pair. A favourite "torture" was to make the children stand on one leg with arms outstretched, holding a bowl of water, if they spilt any water or fell off balance they were beaten. Talking in the dining room could also lead to being locked in a darkened dormitory until midnight or locked in the "black hole", a room at the top of the stairs.

On one occasion Horatio Bottomley refused to get out of bed and was punished by Turner another particularly sadistic member of staff, who used a stick with a tack in it which sunk in and scratched the hand. No one seemed particularly sorry when he left. But others remained, like Puxty who were handy with the cane or administered the punishment of making children stand on a rickety revolving stool in front of their classmates. Whether because of the punishment or from sheer frustration children from time to time made attempts to escape, and sometimes succeeded in running away. On one occasion Horatio Bottomley tied sheets together and ran to his uncle, George Jacob Holyoake, the famous socialist who returned him to Mason, who had him thrashed.

Punishments loom large in the memories, and some recall. Birch rods as the first "instruments of torture", later given up in favour of canes. Sometimes the punishments were made to fit the crime. Being locked in a classroom during a half holiday so that they missed a cricket match. Then on one occasion, when Mr. Read, one of the popular teachers was told that some of the boys had stolen plum pudding, raisins, peas, rock cocoa and had raided the girls' boxes in their playroom, which was out of bounds to them, he charged them with rasing and plundering. He then produced a cane and demanded that the boy concerned should tell who his companions had been, but being made of stern stuff he refused. Mr. Read then asked the others to confess, they did and were then physically punished, locked in a room and given bread and water instead of dinner. However, through the ingenuity of their friends, food was passed to them under the door.

The Smiths had a fearsome reputation, supported unfortunately by J.R. Matthews, who was Mason's first estate secretary, they were in charge of the children outside lesson times, Smith, an ex-Indian Army man, had a great liking for discipline, which was unfortunately of a sadistic kind. His favourite punishment was to line the boys up in sixes, stripped in preparation for baths, as they stood shivering waiting their turn he beat them with a bunch of leather laces or rubber piping. He had an alarming appearance, bearded and stern, never averse to using his hands, fists, feet or a stick, often thrashing the boys for wrong doing. He was the drill master who punished anyone who got out of step, or turned the wrong way. They were woken by him at 6a.m., and anyone who failed to get up following the first call was severely punished. It was even rumoured that he slept with a pistol under his pillow. He was said by the children to be "doolally top", and his wife was not thought to be much better. Following the death of his wife, Smith had to leave, much to the pleasure of all the boys.

Incarcerated within the orphanage walls the children felt the injustice of some of the actions by the staff and when on one "pancake day" they thought they should have a holiday, they went on strike. They crowded round the great oak door and said "If you don't give us a holiday we'll all run away". Mason appeared in the lobby, "You'll all run away will you", he said as he quitely unbolted the door and opened it wide, "Now run away all of you, and get out of my orphanage quick". Suitably rebuked and cowed they all slunk away, the strike was over.

34. Sir Josiah Mason.

But, there were also happy memories of Christmas with full stockings and cards to matron, and Mason handing out gifts from the tree and ship, and singing carols with them. On his birthday they sang songs in his honour and his eyes filled with tears and he said "God bless my children". He appeared then as a benevolent figure, smiling and patting them on the head with his two dogs, Rough and Fluff, at his heels.

Other happy events frequently appear as highlights in the record. The annual outing to Sutton Park was thought to be the greatest day of the year, as this was when most hours were spent outside the orphanage walls. During this trip they went boating, sat on the grass to have refreshments and had an enjoyable day. But the younger children did not go, but went instead to a farm nearby. Another outing during the winter, much enjoyed, was to the cattle show in Birmingham, when they had buns and milk under some arches which were thought to be those of the Town Hall. They were also taken for occasional walks, in the lanes of Erdington and some vividly recalled seeing bicycles, mostly Penny Farthings. Sport was not neglected, cricket and rounders were played, and once a year they played cricket against the local Erdington School, football it appears was in its infancy. May Day saw the children, wreaths on heads, dancing around the Maypole. Many also recalled the sunny afternoons, with the Masons in attendance, when the children were allowed to play games on the lawns. There was also Guy Fawkes night which brought the usual celebrations, with bonfire and fireworks, but only the older boys were allowed out of doors.

The enclosed world of the orphanage served to magnify the more horrendous tales, such as the time Suckpling the engineer went into the kitchen with his hand torn off by machinery. He was later fitted with a hook and found another job by Mason, as a postman in Erdington. His successor did not fare much better when he was called out from his sick bed to repair a burst pipe on a winter's day, contracted penumonia and died.

However, there were excursions into the outside world with walks to Sutton, Walmley and Tyburn, when they looked for glow worms in Bell Lane and were regaled with the story of the Mary Ashford murder. Sometimes the older children were sent on errands to the village post office or one of the few shops. When this favour was bestowed, the lucky child took orders from the others to purchase "goodies" such as liquorice bootlaces and rifleballs, and levied a toll by nibbling the goods, or keeping the change. Some of the greatest excitement was reserved from the twice yearly occasions, when family and friends were allowed to visit. It was a time of great pleasure or could equally be of disappointment if a name was not called to meet visitors.

Days devoted to pleasure were few, but well remembered, most were long and hard. A typical day started at 6a.m., the boys were told to get up and were beaten if not up in five minutes. Then they washed and dressed and worked until breakfast at 8.30a.m. This usually consisted of bread and treacle or occasionally a slice of bacon. Cocoa was served in tin mugs, no cups and saucers. During meal-time talking was not allowed, and after breakfast there were prayers, a hymn and a reading from the Bible. Then school in the morning followed by play at lunchtime, and afternoon school from 2.00-4.00p.m. This was followed by tea which consisted of bread and butter, tea and sometimes cake. Later prayers and bed at 7.30p.m. for the younger children. (35)

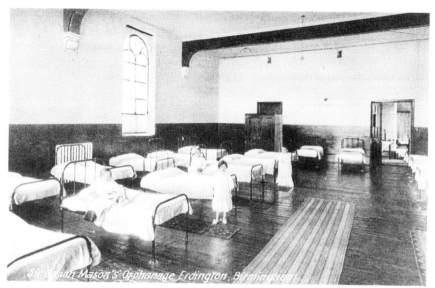

35. Dormitory Mason's Orphanage, Erdington.

There were always regular chores to be done, such as once a week, the stairs from the dormitory had to be scrubbed by two boys, and 250 knives and forks had to be cleaned every Saturday morning. But a more prized job, was to take drinking water in cans from the well to Mason, for often when the children visited Norwood House, they were received kindly and given cake by Mrs. Jefferies, Mason's first servant. They called her granny and she told them stories of her work for Mason, or the master, as she called him. Of how she wrapped a cold dinner in a red handkerchief which he carried as he walked to work, and of how the whole household was excited when he purchased his first pony and trap. She was later pensioned and provided with accommodation in one of Mason's almshouses, and he visited her regularly until her death at the age of 92. Norwood House and gardens was seen as a paradise, and an additional pleasure was a secret hiding place in a hedge near an iron gate in Bell Lane, where Miss Winwood the housekeeper would place an apple or cake for them.

The laundry also provided work, turning the handle of the clothes press - a large box filled will stones. But some work, such as that in the kitchen, offered perks through illicit practices such as removing the soft inside of loaves cooked in large tins by Larkin the baker. Those who recorded such actions justified them, because of need to supplement the orphanage diet.

They all began their chores at 6a.m. in the hope of finishing by lunchtime. But there was other work which added to their burdens - cleaning the hall and kitchen, and cleaning 150 pairs of boots. Some staff particularly those out of sympathy with the boys, took the view that the bigger the boy the harder he should be worked. Sometimes, work provoked prankish gestures, such as flooding the bedroom floors when washing them, so that the water dripped into the class-rooms below, or when washing windows with a hand pump they directed the hose through a broken pane into the girls' classroom.

However, all was not doom and gloom, in their rebellion against the system some of the children banded together and planned a few pranks, which upset the somewhat repressive regime of the orphan-age. One such trick was to let the treacle out of the vat in the kitchen, (36) this not only caused an incredibly sticky mess, but produced problems for the meal planners, as bread and treacle was part of the staple diet, served up regularly for breakfast. These exciting episodes seemed to stimulate the children to greater adven-tures in reckless defiance of authority, which resulted on one occasion in a boy falling into the treacle barrel. Another prank, to test the courage of the children, was to hang on the outside of the stair bannister and climb hand over hand to the top, and then slide down leaning forward with hands above their heads. No doubt exciting but also considered very dangerous. Then when they felt really cold, they defied authority and went for warmth to the drying room, if caught, they were punished and sent to bed and missed the magic lantern show.

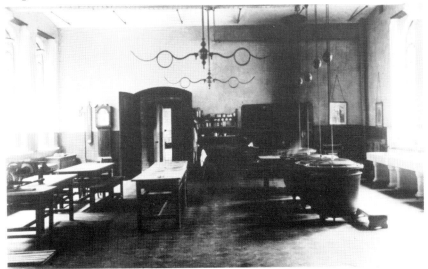

36. Kitchen Mason's Orphanage, Erdington.

More acceptable play took place on the field or in the recreation room. But when the new wing to the orphanage was built the field was no longer available, so they had to make use of the corridor, to play with whips and tops. During the dark evenings the recreation room was dimly lit by a gas jet, and in it was an old chest of drawers which contained the older boys treasurers, but which smelt strongly of orange peel. More formal entertainments included temperance lectures, concerts and occasional visits to Curzon Hall to see Hamilton's Panorama, which included Japanese jugglers and conjurors. Mason took a personal interest in most of these events.

Some of the children were interested in animals and gardening. Their pets included: three jackdaws, doves, two parrots, silkworms, and a tortoise. On one occasion they were told by the matron that they would receive a 1/- (5p), if they found the tortoise, only to learn that it had been given to Dr. Thomas, but no explanation for this action was given. Mason also kept pigs on a farm in the grounds near Norwood House in Bell Lane. Very occasionally they were killed and the children enjoyed the luxury of pork pie for dinner, and "scratching cake" for tea. A piece of ground at the bottom of the playground was divided into plots about three yards square, and were cultivated by fifty of the older boys. Part of this excercise was to form partnerships, a kind of business experience, under which they were allowed to draw money from the bank for seeds, while tools were provided free. Competitions were held with prizes, which on one occasion was an atlas. They most often grew sweet peas, nasturtiums, and mignonette.

Time was devoted to religious services although it was widely known that Mason did not approve of the catechism, articles of faith, sectarian distinctions and prejudices, and put himself down as a "follower of the Lord". To attend services children marched two abreast into the chapel, then waited in silence for Mason. The services held owed much to Wesleyan Methodism, and Mason eventually appointed Rev. Benjamin Wright, the brother-in-law of Alderman Johnson, his solicitor, as chaplain. He was well-liked by the children and secured privileges for some boys to sing carols at his house, where they had a good time. To some of the children these services were important events, when they observed the attendance of visitors and strangers who sat in the gallery. VIP's occupied the front rows of the chapel, and included the trustees, Miss Winwood, Parsons (the coach man) and his family, Mrs. Read and family, Miss Helminster, Miss Griffiths (Mason's niece), and Mason who sat by himself on a hard bench. However, there were hours of boring sermons which led to lots of fidgeting and mischief.

Most of the children looked forward to their food long before the meal times, although the menu barely changed throughout the year. Their favourite dinner was soup and pudding, which they found more satisfying than meat and potatoes. Among their dislikes were the bread and milk, and the bread and treacle served for breakfast. There was very little variety in the diet. Tea was often two pieces of bread and dripping, or sometimes treacle, with a tin mug of cocoa, often Cadbury's Rock Cocoa. They never tasted better porridge or suet pudding, and put this down to the cooking by steam. Sometimes in error an extra piece of bread appeared so they took it in turns to claim it. With twenty boys at each table it averaged out at about, one extra slice, once every two months. Sunday meals varied a little from the weekday ones, particularly when seed cake was served, and they did not have cocoa. Christmas saw greater variety, and additional luxuries which included, an orange and two apples each, provided by Jevons, one of the trustees.

The consensus seemed to be that the food was plain and the portions rather small. Most of the children seemed to thrive and remain healthy - indigestion was unknown. Such was the enthusiasm for the food that the metal cups and plates needed very little washing. (37) Whenever Mason asked if they had enough food they always said yes, as they were afraid of the matron Miss Caroline Stockwin - although her sister Miss Ann was kinder and a favourite with the boys.

37. Dining Hall Mason's Orphanage, Erdington.

Mason was a firm believer in homeopathic medicine. One of the boys recalled being vaccinated from the arm of one of the girls and ending up with lumps on his neck similar to that of the girl. They were also given liberal doses of bella-donna and nux vomica. In contrast to the dentist's visits when Mason gave them sweets and it was said, that some of the children were prepared to have their teeth extracted in order to receive sweets.

There is no doubt that most of the children held Mason in high regard, although they were sometimes in awe of his presence and power. They found it hard to believe that he had knowledge of the sadistic brutality that they were exposed to, or the hard work that they undertook.

One boy's memory of Mason, written many years later, described him as, "a striking personality, tall handsome pink complexion, beautiful white hair and beard, the hair curling upwards from the neck, very prominent blue viens on his temple, wonderful keen, penetrating yet twinkling eyes, very high forehead, very firm mouth, of commanding appearance, a type of man rarely if ever seen today". (38) "He was accompanied by his two dogs Fluff and Rough (possibly Skye Terrier breed) with bells round their necks, they always preceded him so that we knew when he was coming, also from the sound of his thick stick. This prompted all the children to stand and salute".

Another wrote, "I remember many years ago a description by J. Thackray Bunce, "that the children would brighten up at his (Mason's) approach, would run up to him, and put their little hands in his". I never saw that done as we were rather afraid of him, possibly because it was always, "Hush behave yourself Sir Josiah is coming". He would also shake his stick at us and call us young rascals. We misunderstood that action perhaps, as also the twinkle in the stern deep-set eyes".

There was obvious speculation about Mason's motives, with comments such as, "I have been told that he would not have built an orphanage if he had children of his own. And that, he surrounded himself with big men, but I believe he made or helped to make them what they were, men who laid the foundations of the Birmingham of today:- Issac Horton, G.J. Johnson, Dr. Gibbs Blake, Yeomans, Solomon Jevons, Thomas Avery, Elkington, Chance, Holliday, J.A. Cossins, R.W. Dale, Allen, Cooper, Thackray Bunce, and others".

"I have often thought it strange that Mason, a manufacturer, a town man, invested his money in farm lands, country estates et al

38. Sir Josiah Mason.

and one of his trustees Issac Horton, a farmer and pork butcher, invested his in buildings and town properties. Mason a man of no education, poor at thirty years of age, wealthy at fifty", These words were written by George James Lewis who was a resident of the orphanage from 1870 to 1882.

Others remarked on how Mason's deafness made it difficult for them to talk to him, and how this was a particular problem during the last two years of his life. When they took water to his house at midday each day, he asked them questions, often it was, "Do you like being at the orphanage?". They always said, "Yes Sir", not really daring to say otherwise. It must be remembered that they were writing in the early 1930's of their perceptions of Mason when they were children, and also often felt that they owed him a lot.

But when they left it was traumatic, each was given a bible, a change of clothes and a wooden box to put them in. This was usually at the age of fourteen, when most felt ill equipped to cope with the outside world. They had only the merest idea of a life sometimes glimpsed in the houses of the staff. The silvered buttons on the uniform were cut off before they left, but they went out in the easily recognised institution clothes. They were often found jobs. In one instance the chaplain took a boy for an office boy job at the Daily Post at 7/- a week which was 2/- above the normal rate, because he came from the orphanage. Others were apprenticed sometimes without consent. One boy was apprenticed in this way to a barber in a Birmingham salon, for seven years at 3d a week rising in the seventh year fo 2/6d. He worked ninety hours a week including Sundays and a half day on Bank Holidays. It was all too much for him and after a few months he ran away.

Another recalled what started as a happier experience, being employed within the orphanage as an office boy to the secretary, W.T. Davis, described as, "a wise, nervous and affectionate gentleman". Even so, this boy was not excused the heavier work, and described his distaste for scrubbing the dining room floor.

To many of the people who wrote their reminiscences, the orphanage took on a "sacred" quality, which provided character building and discipline necessary to the development of a sound personality. Mason himself was imbued with the characteristics of a loving parent. The reality of the situation was probably closer to the record left by others, of a harsh regime run by a mixture of well meaning and sadistic staff, whose treatment of the children was probably little different from that given to those who lived outside the orphanage; where many children were employed under harsh conditions on farms and in factories. On balance perhaps, for some to be incarcerated within the orphanage walls was preferable to being destitute, ill clothed and shoeless in the streets of Victorian Birmingham. Mason's benevolent philanthropic paternalism may not have been completely altruistic, but his generosity in financial terms cannot be questioned, even if his motives were rather complex. Certainly many people in retrospect felt him, in the main, to have been kind and gentle, in contrast to some of those he employed.

John Hingeley who became secretary of the orphanage sometime after Mason's death, wrote down some of his memories in 1933. It is worth noting some of his comments, which tend to reflect upon changes which took place in the 1880's. These included summer holidays for the children, hanging pictures in the rooms and corridors, arranging entertainments, persuaded the trustees to change the old uniform, all of which attempted to transform the institution into a home. The cirriculum was also changed to give more time for sports and recreation and a swimming pool was built in 1889. Religious services were made more appropriate for the children.

It was thought by some of the former pupils that Mason would not have approved of some of the changes. Particularly children with parents, being admitted to the orphanage, outsiders being educated at the school, and teachers appointed and paid for by Birmingham Education Authority.

Chapter 9
Science College

The idea of creating a scientific and commercial college or a central university had been mooted by Birmingham medical men in the early 1830's and continued by Anglican Clerics at Queen's College into the 1840's. It was probably this influence which contributed to Mason's decision to found an independent establishment, with an insistence that it concentrate on practical knowledge of scientific subjects, excluding mere literary education, and that it should be open to all in the town and the district.

Until the middle of the nineteenth century prevailing influences were firmly against the use of universities for vocational training. Cardnial Newman and J.S. Mill were staunch defenders of the traditional liberal education ideal. It was felt that a university education should not relate to specific employments but should improve the individual by imbuing him with sound principles of policy and religion. Newman was strongly opposed to Mason's lack of religious affiliation, to the point of refusing in July 1882, after Mason's death to inscribe two of his books for the College Library.

The object was not to make skilful lawyers, physicians or engineers, but capable and cultivated human beings. These opinions did not present qualms to the men founding the technological civic universities, least of all Mason, with his striking individuality, and he specifically excluded literary subjects from his college. The chief supporters for sciences, even industrial sciences to be taught in the universities were Herbert Spencer and T.H. Huxley. Huxley, echoing Spencer took up the theme at Birmingham, expressed his support for the new scheme of education, and even Mason's exclusion of literary subjects on the grounds that the sciences were more useful than the classics, and stressed that for attaining "culture" an exclusively scientific education was at least as useful as an exclusively literary one. Birmingham, like Sheffield and Manchester, began with the actions of an individual businessman. Mason as an innovative scientific entrepreneur appreciated as well as Firth, at Sheffield and more than Owens, at Manchester the potential importance of higher scientific education for industry.

In the 1870's Mason began to formulate his plans for an educational project, based on ideas gained from the people around him including G.J. Johnson, his solicitor, who had always suggested a science college. Much of the preparatory work was done in conjunction with Johnson and Dr. J. Gibbs Blake, whom he had persuaded to come to Birmingham to look after the children in the orphanage. It appears that for about ten years, Blake travelled on the continent, using his holiday time to visit technical colleges in Germany, France and Switzerland and later the United States of America. Then Jethro A. Cossins a native of Somerset, and a well known Birmingham architect, made the same trip, so that as an architect he would be aware of the most recent developments in this field. Blake and Johnson became the first trustees and were joined in 1872 by William Costin Aitken, Bunce, George Shaw and Dr. Thomas Pretious Heslop. Johnson, Shaw and Heslop had already been involved in academic life as professors at Queen's College.

Originally Mason had wanted to purchase the building occupied by Queen's College, in Paradise Street. Later he considered adding his college on to the Birmingham and Midland Institute (B.M.I.), but this had been complicated by the need to vary the Institutes Foundation Act through a further Act of Parliament. He did however contribute £250 in 1871, and again in 1872 towards the cost of enlarging the theatre at the B.M.I. He had also become aware that the part-time evening classes at the B.M.I. could not provide enough scientific teaching to meet the rapid advances in science. His views were supported, when following the opening of the college, in 1880, the Natural History Society withdrew from the B.M.I. to a more spacious room of its own in the college.

Eventually his deliberations led to the decision to establish an independent college. Although no land had been purchased, it was agreed that it should be located in the area of Edmund Street and Paradise Street, in the centre of Birmingham. Obtaining the land proved to be a complex business. He first tried to purchase land at the corner of Congreve and Edmund Street through to Great Charles Street but progress was slow as the site was covered with "a network of dingy and dirty passageways and courts". With such a valuable site this meant a whole range of freeholders, leaseholders and sub-tenants. These complex arrangements contributed to slow progress, which were only finally resolved with the assistance of Mason's friends, Horton the property developer who persuaded landowners to sell, and Philip Henry Muntz, M.P. one of the principal landowners. With the land that he had previously purchased close to the Town Hall, and the additional acre plot fronting Edmund Street and Great Charles Street the site was complete. A sketch design of the college was drawn up by Jethro A. Cossins the architect, probably for the laying of the foundation stone, on 23 February, 1875. When it came to building, Mason would have nothing to do with the contract system, instead, the builder Hodgkiss, who happened to be a relative of Mason's by marriage, handled the assignment under the day to day supervision of the architect and his staff.

The Foundation Deed had been formally agreed on the 12 December, 1870, between Mason, Gibbs Blake and Johnson. The document had been perpared by Johnson, and J.B. Braithwaite, Lincoln's Inn. Deeds of Foundation had to follow certain procedures, which Mason had experienced with his orphanage. Then on the 15 December it was enrolled in Chancery where it had to remain for 12 months to comply with the Statutes of Mortmain. Mason followed his previous experience and bequeathed all the endowments of the college to the then Mayor of Birmingham, Thomas Avery, without his knowledge. The following letter being held for twelve months to comply with statute.

Erdington, Birmingham.
December 10 1870

Mr dear Mr. Thos. Avery,

By a codicil to my will dated the 8th December I have bequeathed to you absolutely some freehold and leasehold property in Lancaster Street, Princip Street, Cliveland Street, Steelhouse Lane, Edmund Street and Great Charles Street.... The two latter properties I intend for the site of a College and Schools for technical education and instruction and the other properties towards endowment for which I intend to make further provision by my will.

The object and purpose of the Institution are fully detailed in a trust deed which I hope shortly to execute, but in case of my death before such deed can be perfected according to the Statute of Mortmain I have given this property to you in full confidence that you will deal with it as I should have done if living.

I am my dear Mr. Thos. Avery

Faithfully yours

Josiah Mason

The letter had to be handed to Avery in the event of Mason's death. He was Mayor in 1867, and on two subsequent occasions, the last in 1881. Despite his involvement in public life he was able to give time to Mason's College, and in fact left £2,000 to the college in his will.

Work had also commenced on the college cirriculum. Mason was assisted in this task by his friend and legal adviser Johnson, George Shaw formerly Professor of Chemistry at Queen's College and J.T. Bunce. The intention was to provide a system of education which met the practical, mechanical and artistic requirements of the industrial manufacturers of the Midlands, excluding literary and theological pursuits. The following subjects were to be included, Mathematics (abstract and applied), Physics (mathematical and experimental), Chemistry (theoretical, practical and applied), Natural Sciences (geology, mineralogy, with application to mines and metallurgy) and Biology, Botany and Zoology (with special application to manufacturers), Physiology (with special application to health), and Engineering, subsequent deeds added English, French and German. Any other subjects could be included if they met the intentions of the founder. At a later date the cirruculum was extended to allow courses leading to degrees in the Victoria Federal University of Leeds, Liverpool and Manchester, or any other University the College formed part of. However, Theology and Politics were still excluded. Further stipulations of the deed were that admission to popular classes should not be refused on the grounds of creed, race, age, sex or birthplace. However, for regular classes all other things being equal the trustees were to give preference to pupils from the orphanage of up to one fifth of pupils. Although this was not always the experience of those who tried to gain entrance. Then preference was given to eligible candidates from Birmingham and Kidderminster in the ratio 2:1; Students had to be between the age of 14-25, exceptionally they could be over 25, but should not be greater than ratio 10:1.

The trustees had to appoint four professors - one of mathematics, one of physics, one of chemistry, and one of biology, including botany and zoology. The salary of each professor was to be £250 per annum, plus, in each case one half of the class fees. The professors of chemistry and physics were each to be provided with an assistant, at an annual salary of £100.

Mason by excluding literary education and instruction showed his comtempt for literary attainments which were not strictly utilitarian. This was referred to in his obituary to the effect that, "His was, in fact, by no means a literary soul. He seldom if ever figured as a speechmaker, much less as a writer. But upon the value of literary studies and of exercise in the higher and more refined walks of the mind he was by no means fitted to judge. His shrewd business talents enabled him to amass a princely fortune, which, to his honour be it said, he disposed of in a way excellently calculated to benefit the community at large; and if it be true, as is said, that his workmen could never love him, but rather despised his constant exhibitions of stinginess and mean qualities, these and many other private failings are overshadowed and obliterated by the magnitude of those philanthropic efforts which were the result of his labours".

One provision in the last supplement deed is worthy of note, namely, that the trustees had power, when necessary, to alter the courses of teaching and the arrangements of the institution, and they were required at intervals of fifteen years to take these into consideration, with a view to such revision as might seem desirable.

In September 1872 the trustees were increased to six, Blake, G.J. Johnson, William Costen Aitken, John Thackray Bunce, Thomas Pretious Heslop and George Shaw. The first meeting and the signing of the deed took place at Mason's home Norwood House, Erdington. It was signed in the picture gallery on the 23 February, 1873, his 78th birthday. The plans were approved in 1874. (39)

Exactly two years later on his 80th birthday the foundation stone was laid by Mason - by then Sir Josiah, following his knighthood in 1872 - because of heavy snow and frost the ceremony was short. The event was attended by a number of dignitaries, including the M.P. John Bright. In the absence of the Mayor of Birmingham, Joseph Chamberlain, due to his wife's death, Mr Biggs, the Deputy Mayor, made a speech, thanked Mason, and wished him well on his birthday. It is perhaps interesting to note, that although Mason and Chamberlain's work was closely linked through the college, there is no evidence that they ever met.

John Bright, in his speech, appeared to encapsulate the general sentiments with these words:- "I am sorry to say I know very little of Sir Josiah's former life. I know him by what I have seen and heard only recently, but he has acquired for himself a position we don't envy, I am sure, but which we can admire and respect. He has not in the course of his life done some things some men have done to procure fame. He has not led brave or reckless men to battle or to death, as is done sometimes for objects unworthy of the sacrifice. He has not probably - though I am not speaking decidedly on this point, but he has not as far as I know - written a great book. He has not probably given to us an immortal poem that will charm and instruct to the latest generations; but whether you consider these institutions dealing with the orphan and the fatherless, or this institution of today, which will make science the common heritage of the people, he has done that, I say, which will give him a name that will be revered in hundreds and thousands of homes. He has shown himself the helper of the forlorn and the helpless, the promoter of that science, of those branches of science especially, upon which we know the future prosperity of your city must be built. I am here to offer my tribute of respect and admiration to one whom we now deem, and one who will by generations to come be deemed, one of the worthiest of the worthy citizens of this great city.

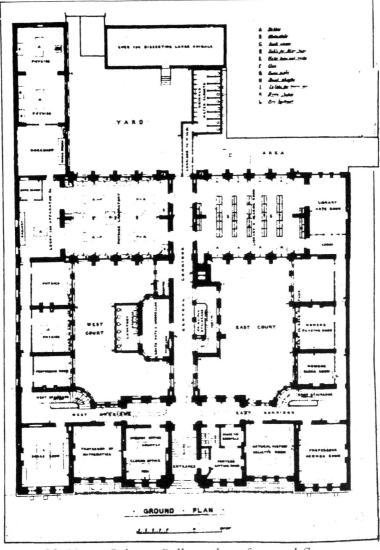

39. Mason Science College plan of ground floor.

Mason in his reply, read by Bunce, expressed his wish to provide sicentific education for all classes of people in Birmingham and Kidderminster linked to industrial work in the area. He also said, "Trusting that I who have never been blessed with children of my own may yet in these students leave behind me an intelligent, earnest, industrious truth loving and truth seeking progeny".

The building was eventually completed on the 23 February, 1880, and was formally opened on the 1 October, 1880. (40) The ceremony began with a meeting at the Town Hall, presided over by Richard Chamberlain, Mayor of Birmingham. Members of Birmingham and Kidderminster council were present, as were the leading scientific and literary figures from Birmingham and the Universities of Oxford, Cambridge and London, and the Victoria Federal University. The Birmingham Festival Choral Society sang Mendelsohn's hymn, "Let Our Theme of Praise Ascending", and performed other works for the assembled group.

40. Mason Science College, Birmingham.

Then an address was given by Professor Thomas Henry Huxley, who asked, among other things, that arts subjects, including sociology be included in the cirriculum. Lunch was then provided at

91

the Queen's Hotel. Then at 7 o'clock in the evening a "Conversazione", attended by a thousand people was held at the college, and they were received by Mason in the reception room. As part of the opening ceremony Mason handed the key of the college to Johnson saying, "The key of my college is now mine, and I can say that the college is mine, but in a moment I shall be able to say so no longer, for I now present it, and with it the college, to my old friend, Mr. Johnson, on behalf of my trustees, to be held by them in trust for the benefit of generations to come". (41) The whole building was elaborately decorated and furnished, and included some fine enamels by Elkington & Co. A programme of instrumental and vocal music, dancing, exhibitions and refreshments, accompanied the proceedings. As an added attraction electric light was used to illuminate the entrance hall and principal corridors. As the use of electricity for lighting was in its infancy this was seen as an exciting innovation. Again Joseph Chamberlain, now President of the Board of Trade was absent. Ironic in some ways, in view of his later enthusiastic involvement in transferring the college into a university. But perhaps understandable in view of their earlier conflicting business interests, when Mason tried to take over Nettlefold and Chamberlain's screw company, a move which upset Chamberlain very much. Chamberlain was also unhappy about Mason's approach to education, and made disparaging comments about his Science College. However, other people lavished praise on Mason, on this occasion, and again in March 1881 when he recieved and illuminated address from the first students of the college.

On the 2 October the following description of Mason's Science College appeared in the Birmingham Daily Post:- "The site extends from Edmund Street to Great Charles Street about 1 acre, with 150' frontage to the former street, and a depth of 313', only half the ground at present is covered with buildings. Arranged round two quadrangles, the main block fronting to Edmund Street, and a building of about the same size standing parallel with it at the rear, are connected by East and West wings by a covered central corridor and out offices which divided the enclosed space into two open courts. With the exception of the East wing all the building is four storeys in height, and in the centre of the principal facade a large musem has been provided partly in the lofty roof space. Walls of brick and stone, form the front in Edmund Street, deep red brick from Kingswinford, with Portland, Bath and Bolton Wood stone for the windows and other details.

41. *Mason College opening ceremony, 1st October, 1880. Mason handing key to Johnson.*

The elevation is symmetrical with the principal entrance in the centre in 13th Century style with details of a somewhat French character. The ground floor is 7 feet above street level, and a massive plinth of Bromley stone is carried to this height. The western gable extremity of the principal front has not been completed because of a dispute about light. (A matter later settled by the purchase of an adjoining building).

The college is entered from a boldly moulded and deeply recessed arch with shafts of grey York stone. The entrance is closed by a wrought iron gate. On the front at the top of the central gable, 122 feet above Edmund Street is the crest of the founder". Another paper, The Daily Mail commented, "As a specimen of Gothic architecture, it is one of the finest the town possesses". (42) (43)

Mason contributed £170,000 towards this project. An endowment of £100,000 and £60,000 towards building costs. The endowment properties conveyed to the original trustees were added to in 1881, and consisted of freehold lands, buildings and ground rents in various parts of Birmingham providing revenue of £3,700 p.a. with a capital value of £110,000 plus £60,000 provided by Mason. According to the cash book the income from rents and leases between 1876 and 1883 was £3,438.11s.10d.

42. *Mason University College Council room with half length Munn's portrait of Mason, 1897.*

43. *Mason University College Physics Laboratory, 1897.*

Despite all his generosity, Mason always insisted on the best possible bargain, as the comments which followed the purchase of the Ketley fossil collection for the college illustrate. Samuel Allport the curator wrote, "Sir Josiah has been here this morning, and is now quite satisfied. The old habit of making the best possible bargain will no doubt last to the end".

The college trustees were also named as his residuary legatees, and after his death were increased by empowering Birmingham Town Council to nominate five trustees, who need not be members of the Council, but must be laymen and Protestants. This was confirmed in Council Minutes of 5 July, 1881, following a letter to the Mayor, Joseph Chamberlain from Johnson on behalf of the trustees.

Once again Mason used the mermaid, (44) with the motto, "Progress through Knowledge", as his personal stamp of approval upon this achievement. Maurice Cheesewright states that, "The mermaid with the mirror and comb was Mason's heraldic crest borrowed from an earlier and apparently unrelated Mason of Greenwich - without authority, according to Fox-Davies's Complete Guide to Heraldry. She thus found her way into the Mason College badge and the University of Birmingham Coat of Arms. She was evidently as much an object of affection to Mason as she has been to a century of students, for her figure in stone perched on the pinnacle of Mason's College, remained there for 85 years; she was then rescued and re-erected, minus arms, in the foyer of the Students Union".

44. Statue of mermaid minus arms from Mason College now in foyer of Students' Union, University of Birmingham.

The college attracted its share of famous people, including Constance Naden, a brilliant student who became a poet, and Karl Dammann former German Master at King Edward's School who became Professor of German Language and Literature in 1881. Then two students who were destined to become future Prime Ministers, Neville Chamberlain sent there by his father to learn about science, metallurgy and engineering, and at about the same time Alfred Baldwin sent his son Stanley for a session of lectures.

One of the first professors appointed was Dr. J.H. Poynting, one of the most prominent and inspirers of intellectual life and learning in Birmingham. Another influential figure was the Rev. Crosskey, a Unitarian minister who introduced teacher training into the college, and campaigned for university status.

After a decade of gradually increased co-operation, the Medical Faculty of Queen's College became part of Mason's College in 1892. Queen's College left with only its theological department became a school for the training of clergy. By 1898, Mason's College had become Mason's University College, and control passed from the trustees appointed by Mason to a Court of Governors drawn from throughout the Midlands but dominated by Joseph Chamberlain.

Negotiations continued, with the support of many prominent politicians and local leaders, in an effort to establish a university. Progress was made on the 3 June, 1897, when the Royal Assent was given to the Mason University College Act. Following in Mason's philanthropic footsteps Carnegie gave £50,000 towards the endowment fund in 1899. Then Lord Calthorpe gave a 25 acre site at the south west corner of Edgbaston, and afterwards a further 20 acres for athletic purposes, and an anonymous gift of £59,000 provided the Clock Tower. On 24 March, 1900, the University of Birmingham was born by Royal Charter granted by Queen Victoria.

A few months later, Joseph Chamberlain, Chancellor of the University wrote to Henry Duke of Norfolk, Earl Marshall and Head of College of Arms applying for a grant of Arms, and this was awarded on the 27 August, 1900. "A lion rampant with two heads in sinister a mermaid holding in the dexter hand a mirror and in the sinister a comb". Most of this, as Christine Penney reminds us, had come from the boys at the orphanage who had on their electroplated button badge a two headed lion on a shield, and the girls who had a mermaid on their belt buckle, both had the motto, "Deeds of Love". Edward VII formally opened the new university on 7 July, 1909.

Lucy Taylor in her short biography of Mason, projects Victorian optimism, pride and a sense of permanence bestowed on their buildings, with the comment, "And this fine building one of the ornaments of the City of Birmingham, is not only magnificent and imposing, but is in every way suited to the purpose for which it is intended, and built, moreover, of such excellent material that the busy destroyer, time will have to expend a good many centuries of it before it can show signs of decay or insecurity". Despite this optimism, the college buildings were demolished between January and September 1964 to make way for the Paradise Circus redevelopment. Mason's College being replaced by the new Central Library building. A plaque (45) on the wall of the forum, below the library, is now the only indication of the grand building, symbol of scientific education and forerunner of the university, which once occupied the site.

45. *Plaque in forum below Central Library, Birmingham, marking site of Mason College.*

Chapter 10
Public Image and Power

Although Mason did not enter into public life to any major extent, he was not alone in this, examples exist of entrepreneurs such as Thomas Coghlan Horsfall in Manchester, and Charles Mander in Wolverhampton, all powerful local "notables" who shunned public life.

In Mason's case evidence exists of his involvement with a few ad hoc committees and companies. One such was his support for a railway line through Erdington. There were two different proposals which tended to divide the community. Some supported the Eastern Line leaving the Midland Railway at Saltley crossing to Gravelly Hill, with a station at Mason Road near the village green and one near Mason's Orphanage on Chester Road, another at Maney and the terminus just off the parade in Sutton Coldfield. The rival Western Line was to run west of the Birmingham Road. Mason had been a member of the provisional committee set up in September 1857 to consider a railway line but once the East West rivalry developed he aligned himself with the supporters of the Eastern Line. It is uncertain how actively he was involved with this committee, but he was not among the list of regular attenders. This proposal was of greater advantage to him because of its close proximity to his land, and proposed orphanage. Public meetings were held, petitions and counter petitions were signed, M.P.'s were solicited. Parliamentary Bills were eventually presented and the rival proposals financially supported to the tune of £60,000 each. A Select Committee of the House of Commons deliberated on the rival Bills from the 4-7 July, 1859, and finally with the support of the London North Western Railway the Western Line was adopted. In a schedule to the Act there is a description of Mason's land holding affected by the proposed plan. (46)

A more critical association was with the Birmingham Banking Company, Mason was involved both as customer and shareholder. He was in good company as Birmingham Council also banked there. It had been a thriving concern from 1824 - with the public company set up in 1829 - under the management of the talented and famous Paul Moon James. It was reputed to have been for a time the largest bank in Birmingham. However, in 1866, along with a number of other banks, it failed to survive a financial crisis. Moon had by this time moved on to another banking appointment in Manchester. He had been succeeded by William Beaumont until his death in June 1863, when his son W.H. Beaumont, who had previously acted as sub-manager was appointed and held office until 30 April, 1866. Mr. Shaw then became general manager on the 13 June, and E.N.S. Rouse became manager, positions they held until the bank stopped payment.

Birmingham, Erdington, & Sutton=Coldfield Railway.

CAPITAL £60,000,

IN 6,000 SHARES OF £10 EACH.—DEPOSIT £1 PER SHARE.

The Liability of the Shareholders will be limited by the Act to the amount of their Shares.

Provisional Directors.

Chairman—SIR JOHN RATCLIFF, Mayor of Birmingham.

Deputy Chairman—BARON D. WEBSTER, ESQ., Penns Sutton-Coldfield.

JOSIAH MASON, ESQ. Erdington, Birmingham.
THOS. S. CHEVASSE, ESQ., Wylde Green, Sutton-Coldfield.
ABRAHAM DIXON, ESQ., Birches Green, Birmingham.
G. R. ELKINGTON, ESQ., Birmingham.
CHARLES SHAW, ESQ., Edgbaston, Birmingham.

WILLIAM FOWLER, ESQ., Birches Green, Birmingham.
ZACCHEUS WALKER, ESQ., Birmingham.
GEORGE BODDINGTON, ESQ., Driffield House, Sutton-Coldfield.
ABEL ROLLASON, ESQ., Shepherd's Green House, Erdington.

With power to add to their number.

Bankers.

THE BIRMINGHAM AND MIDLAND BANKING COMPANY, Birmingham.

Engineer.

JAMES B. BURKE, ESQ.

Solicitor

W. F. MANNING, ESQ.,
20, Great George Street, Westminster.

Local Solicitors.

Messrs. HOLBECHE & ADDENBROOKE,
Sutton-Coldfield.

Secretary.

MR. EDWARD CARTER.

46. Company details Birmingham, Erdington and Sutton Coldfield Railway, Mason listed as one of provisional directors.

The day this and other banks ceased business was known in Birmingham as "Black Saturday", and although efforts were made to revive the bank at a meeting of directors and shareholders, including Mason, on August 3, 1866, the attempt failed when the proposal was put to the vote. Neverthless when a new bank was formed, it included Mason from among the old directors appointed to the new board, some of Mason's associates such as Isaac Horton, J.B. Elkington, and Frederick Elkington, were included on the provisional committee, and his solicitors also acted for the Bank. The amount of capital to be raised was £1,500,000 in 30,000 shares or £50 each, but it was only intended to call up £10 per share. Mason then became, for a short time the chairman, and it prospered despite the difficulties experienced by its predecessor, (47).

At a meeting of shareholders on 24 March, 1869, the report of the investigating committee into the collapse of the original bank was received, and appeared in the Post of that date. In a very detailed report concern was expressed about the management, bad debts and the resignation of W.H. Beaumont on the 23 April, 1866, for what he stated, was an offer of alternative employment more suited to his health. There were also references to Beaumont's defective book-keeping and dishonoured bills.

In the Post of 3 March, 1869, there was a report of the unfortunate suicide of J.A. Beaumont, a solicitor aged 36, a widower with two children who was the brother of W.H. Beaumont former manager of the Birmingham Banking Company. He was found in his bedroom with his throat cut. The account mentions, "The unfortunate connection of the deceased as solicitor of the former Birmingham Banking Company".

A report in the Ironmonger of 31 August, 1866, states, "The public are still in the dark as to the real causes which brought about the disastrous failure of the Birmingham Banking Company. The first meetings of shareholders and depositors were calm and dispassionate, while there remained a hope of resuscitating, or at least "making a market" of the old concern. A new venture styled "The Birmingham Banking Company Limited", was launched, the shares duly allotted, and the goodwill and premises of the old bank having been purchased, a new limited liability bank was opened for business on the 9th inst. Mr. Josiah Mason has been elected chairman, and Mr. W.M. Warden (Warden and Sons, iron merchants) deputy chairman of the new company". There was no further evidence of Masons's involvement with the bank.

Birmingham Banking Company

LIMITED.

To be incorporated under The Companies' Act, 1862, which limits the liability of each Shareholder to the amount of his Shares.

CAPITAL, £1,500,000, in 30,000 Shares of £50 each.

Deposit, £1 10s. per Share on application, and £1 10s. on allotment; £1 in one month, and £1 in two months after allotment.

No subsequent Call to exceed £2 10s. per Share, at intervals of not less than three months.

It is not intended to call up more than £10 per Share.

Provisional Committee.

YATES, EDWIN, Esq., Mayor of Birmingham.
ATKINS, Mr. JAMES, Cambridge Street Works.
AVINS, JOHN, Highfield House, Moseley.
BOLTON, Mr. WILLIAM, Hagley Road.
BRINSLEY, Mr. ALDERMAN, Harborne.
BROWNING, Mr. CHARLES LLOYD, Weoley Park, Birmingham.
CATTELL, Mr. THOMAS, Corn Merchant, Birmingham.
CHRISTIAN, Mr. HENRY, Harborne.
CLIFT, Mr. J. E., Redditch.
COOKSEY, H. R., Esq., Oak Mount, Edgbaston.
DAVENPORT, Mr. EDWARD, Gravelly Hill.
DAVENPORT, Mr. ROBERT, George Street, Edgbaston.
EDELSTEN, Mr. PETER, The Woodlands, Edgbaston
EVANS, Mr. JOHN, Aston Brook Mill.
ELKINGTON, Mr. J. B., Newhall Street, Birmingham.
ELKINGTON, FREDERICK, Esq., Northfield.
FINDON, F. J., Esq., Prestbury, Cheltenham.
GUEST, Mr. JOSEPH, Ashted.
HOLLIDAY, WILLIAM, Esq., New Street, Birmingham.
HORTON, Mr. JOSHUA, Smethwick.
HOLLOWAY, Mr. DANIEL, Auctioneer, Yardley.
HOPKINS, Mr. J. H., Calthorpe Street.
HORTON, Mr. ISAAC, Spiceal Street.
LLOYD, Mr. RICHARD, New Street, Birmingham.
LOWE, Mr. HENRY, Norfolk Road, Edgbaston.
LUCAS, Mr. EDWARD, Mount Street, Birmingham.
LOVERIDGE, Mr. WILLIAM, Erdington Hall.
MASON, JOSIAH, Esq., Erdington.
MANLY, Mr. JOHN, Jun., Chad Hall, Edgbaston.
MILLWARD, Mr. EZRA JAMES, Gun Barrel Maker, Birmingham.
MORGAN, Mr. T. H., Shireland Hall, Birmingham.
MESSENGER, Mr. SAMUEL, Edgbaston.
MADELEY, Mr. RICHARD, Berwood House, Erdington.
PONCIA, JOHN, Esq., Edgbaston.
PINCHES, Mr. HENRY, Leamington.
SCOTT, Mr. W. J. B., Queen's Hotel, Birmingham.
SCOTT, Mr. JOSEPH, Gravelly Hill.
SHACKEL, Mr. JOHN, Small Heath.
STUBBS, JOHN, Esq., Leamington.
TUNSTALL, EDWIN, Esq., Plate Glass Works, Smethwick.
UNITE, Mr. GEORGE, Well Head, Birchfield.
WARDEN, Mr. W. MARSTON, Westbourne Road.
WALKER, Mr. SAMUEL, Hagley Road.
WOODHILL, Mr. J. C., Charlotte Road, Edgbaston.
WALKER, Mr. ZACCHEUS, Acock's Green.
WATSON, Mr. JAMES, Hagley Road, Edgbaston.

With power to add to their number.

Solicitors.

Messrs. TYNDALL, JOHNSON, and TYNDALL,
,, ... and MILWARD, } Birmingham.

THE MEMBERS OF THE BIRMINGHAM STOCK EXCHANGE.

Temporary Offices.

EXCHANGE BUILDINGS, CORNER OF STEPHENSON PLACE, BIRMINGHAM.

Secretaries (pro tem).

Mr. THOMAS F. SHAW.   Mr. HENRY ALLBUTT.

Deposits on Shares received between the hours of 9 and 6 daily, at the Temporary Offices, Exchange Buildings.

47. *Birmingham Banking Company details listing Mason on provisional committee.*

Other incursions by Mason into public life were as a member of the Erdington Turnpike Trust, and a trustee of the Birmingham Homeopathic Hospital, towards which he made a generous donation of £1,000 in 1866. His involvement with the Turnpike Trust appears more mysterious, as he does not seem to have been so generous or active in its support, and is not included in the list of regular attenders.

Always a firm believer in homeopathic remedies Mason was, in 1860, a trustee of the Birmingham Homeopathic Hospital. It had been set up as a small dispensary in Great Charles Street, and moved in May 1847 to more convenient premises in the Old Square. The trustees in 1860 were Edwin Bullock, R.L. Chance, Henry Christian, A. Dixon, Josiah Mason and Henry Van Wart and Dr. Gibbs Blake, who was also one of the medical officers. The new hospital had become necessary because of an increased demand for this form of treatment. In a report of 1866 it was said that, "In consequence of the munificent offers by Mr. Mason and Mr. R.L. Chance to contribute £1,000 each towards the erection of a new building, but because of a disastrous monetary crisis it was not conducive to ask for public subscriptions". Mason and Chance agreed to deposit the money in the bank for the building fund. In 1873 the appeal was re-opened and the two men agreed to increase their donations to £1,500 for building on a site in Easy Row. Mason once again showed enthusiasm for a cause in which he had a personal interest and belief. (48)

48. Homeopathic Hospital, Easy Row, Birmingham.

102

These excursions into public works and institutions, give some insight into Mason's indentification with causes with which he had direct involvement. He banked with the Birmingham Banking Company, moved goods along the Turnpike Roads, was committed to Homeopathic Medicine, and his property would benefit from the railway. It appears from this that his excursions into relevant institutions, gave greater personal advantage and satisfaction, and were considered preferable to power gained through national or local politics, or in the government of the town or its parishes.

However, his wealth was a source of power, and also contributed towards the establishment of personal authority. An examination of his Will, and the endowments of the orphanage and science college, give an indication of large land holdings, and substantial income derived from his industrial concerns. As far as can be ascertained much of his income was invested in land, predominantly in Birmingham and the West Midlands, but also as far afield as Ilford in Essex. This interest in land purchase began as early as 1822, when he was one of the first members of the Summer Place Land Society in Kidderminster, whose members paid a fixed monthly sum, and to whom houses were allocated by ballot.

There appeared to be no clear pattern to his land purchase, no consolidation of holdings to form a large estate, although he owned large parcels of land at Erdington which surrounded his home, Norwood House, and the orphanage nearby. He also owned land and property in central Birmingham. This hapazard pattern of land purchase seems to suggest that most of these transactions were for investment or business purposes.

Wealth brought close contact with a number of influential people, and a study of Mason's friends and associates indicate a large number of interconnected contacts throughout the business, charitable and local political community. Difficulties are encountered in attempting to differentiate between friends and associates, although references show a close relationship with Dr. Gibbs Blake (49) his medical adviser, and G.J. Johnson his solicitor. An analysis of the influence of these associates through their involvement with local organisations, (see appendix 3) gives some indication of their cumulative power.

George James Johnson was the son of George Johnson a manufacturer. He was born in Birmingham on the 10 September, 1826, and lived at Hagley Road. Educated privately he succeeded to the bar in 1855, following being articled to Messrs. Tyndall and Son, Birmingham. He was involved with many local institutions including

Mason's business and charitable enterprises, and was active as a J.P. Perhaps the most important of all Johnson's public work was with the Mason foundations.

Mason's friend and biographer Bunce, (50) was the editor of the Daily Post from 1862, and for the following thirty six years. He had come to Birmingham at the age of nine, from his birth place at Farringdon, in Berkshire, where he was born on the 11 April, 1828, and devoted much of his life to work with public institutions. But he was also involved with a number of other organisations including the Midland Institute, and Free Libraries in 1860. With G.J. Johnson he was consulted by Mason on the foundation of Mason's College, and was one of the first trustees appointed in 1872. He was actively involved in the management of the college and its absorption into a university. Among his many historical works was the "Life of Josiah Mason".

49.
Dr. J. Gibbs Blake, Mason's
friend and medical advisor.

50.
J. Thackray Bunce, Mason's
biographer, friend and advisor
editor of Birmingham
Daily Post.

Of the people for whom there is a recorded connection with Mason, emphasis was focused on 25 who had the opportunity of being directly influenced by him. The power and influence exerted by this group, on the government and industry of Birmingham, exposes the extent of the network open to Mason's influence.

They present as a diverse group of people who represented the arts, local government, medicine, religion and industry. However, there was some commonality. Eighteen were either trustees of the orphanage or science college, or were in some form of business partnership with Mason. The remaining seven had contacts with him over a period of time, either through land transactions, or common committee membership. Seven were prominent members of the Town Council and five, Avery, Beale, Johnson, Pollack (51) and P.H. Muntz held Mayoral office.

L.H. Elkington

T.P. Heslop

G.J. Johnson

M. Pollack

51.   Associates of Mason.

Some of the group were members of the Free Library, hospital committees, particularly that of Queen's Hospital, and held common political party and religious affiliations. Eleven belonged to the Liberal Party and five were non-conformists. There was also an inner group of influential people close to Mason. These were Aitken, Gibbs Blake, Bunce, Heslop, Johnson and Shaw, who provided friendship, professional advice and guidance, and acted as trustees for the orphanage, science college and his pen factory. They were also influential in other aspects of Birmingham life, particularly medicine, education, the law and politics.

Heslop was foremost among them in the medical profession. Thomas Pretious Heslop was born in the West Indies in 1823, of a Scottish father and an Irish mother. In 1848 he graduated in medicine from Edinburgh University and was appointed as the house physician at the General Hospital, Birmingham. He was Bailiff of Mason's College, and gave £6,000 to establish the library there, with 11,000 volumes. He died suddenly on the 17 June, 1885. Following his death a fund was established in his memory to provide scholarships to Mason's College for pupils of King Edward's Schools.

Mason saw himself not so much as the owner, but as the steward of his wealth. But other people's perceptions of him are perhaps a better assessment of his "charisma", and need of an enhanced status. There were the public tributes by individuals such as John Bright, M.P., who on the occasion of the opening of the science college praised "the far seeing liberality of the founder of the college". Further acknowledgement was the request by popular demand of the Town Council for a portrait, and statue, for public display, both of which were eventually provided. Recognition in these instances gave an indication of his status as an entrepreneur and philanthropist.

However, a rather confusing account of Mason's early days of prosperity by Willert Beale in the first edition of the Illustrated Midland News, published in 1890, states that during his early success, Mason's house had been crammed with money in purses, old stockings and other containers, placed under the floorboards, mattresses, up the chimney, and in every nook and cranny. What credence can be given to this is uncertain, but it is true that at the time retail banking was in its infancy. However, the tale continues that during one Christmas, Mason and his wife divided a considerable sum between them, and paid them into separate bank accounts. Perhaps this is based on the first visit he made to his solicitor, Palmer, dressed in his white apron and paper cap he gave the impression of having come to borrow money. Palmer was therefore very surprised when he indicated that he wished to invest £3,000, but nontheless agreed that he would find him some good mortgages.

Perhaps Mason's intention was to establish whether he had yet accumulated four or five thousand pounds. The sum he had agreed with his wife he would need to retire. She had become increasingly concerned about his health, and anxious that it should not deteriorate with the stress of his business activities. Whether the banking story is true or not there is evidence enough that Mason was now an established industrialist. Far from being ready to retire he was looking around for other ways of expending his energies and money, and had already invested in land and property.

But increased concerns about his health persisted. It was at this point that his wife thought that a country residence was the answer, and they took a house in Harborne Road, Edgbaston, Birmingham - considered a country suburb in the 1830's. It was obvious that Mason lived the life of a gentleman, and acquired property to match his status. A directory entry for 1835, shows Mason living in Harborne Road, Edgbaston, and an entry in the Great Levy Book, refers to the property which had a garden, gighouse and stable, on which they paid 11/- (55p) rates in 1835. This was based on 6d. (2½p) in the pound for relief of the poor and other purposes. At that time there were just three other houses in the road, but the number had increased considerably by 1836 and the rates had gone up to 22/11d. However, they did not settle very happily in their new home. So Mason purchased 70 acres of land off the Bristol Road at 'Griffin's Hill, Northfield and built a new home, Woodbrooke. (52) It is difficult to know whether this was another attempt to move to a healthier environment. They remained here until the house was sold to G.R. Elkington in 1842. Many years later, by the gift of George Cadbury, it became the first of the Selly Oak Colleges.

Bunce states that during the period 1839-40 they moved to Slade House, Slade Lane, Erdington. This house built in 1820, and described as a fine Georgian house has been considerably altered over the years, and since 1919 has housed the Brookvale Social Club, and carries the address 9, Anchorage Road, Erdington. However, a relative states in some handwritten comments on Bunce's biography that this is an error, and that they lived during this time at Berwood, (53) Chester Road, Erdington, while Norwood House their final home, was being built in Bell Lane. Their actual residence during this period has not been established, but the length of time would have allowed them to have lived at both addresses.

52. *Woodbrooke, Northfield, Birmingham, built by Mason in 70 acres of ground around 1839.*

53. *Berwood, Chester Road, Erdington where it is claimed the Masons stayed while Norwood House was being built - 1849.*

"Berwood House" stood at 829, Chester Road, described as a good Regency period building. It was renovated in the 1950's and used by Tube Investments. Until 1961 a smaller house of an earlier period stood on the site and was used as kitchens for the main building, all have now been demolished.

Norwood House, (54) his final residence, was built on land between Holly Lane, Silver Birch Road, Bell Lane (Orphanage Road) and Sutton Road. It was described as unpretentious in appearance in accordance with the wishes of the owner. It was well planned, solid, comfortable, well heated and ventilated. Mason's own room was at the front of the house; a modest room well stocked with books, objects and momentos of his business, and portraits of himself and friends. In a prominent position on the mantlepiece was a bust of Samuel Hahemann, founder of homeopathy. By all accounts the rooms were always in a neat state as he was very methodical and could find any document without difficulty. The remainder of the house consisted of comfortable dining room, large drawing room which opened into a picture gallery, containing a unique Viennese self acting organ, which played selections from the great classical masters. Following his death and in accordance with his wishes the organ was placed in the examination room of Mason's College. On the side of the house was a terrace which led down to ornamental grounds and meadows. At the back of the house were greenhouses and a vinery which provided Mason with his famous grapes which he delighted in sending to friends. The gardens were laid out with flower beds in lawns which formed a multi-coloured pattern.

54. Norwood House, Erdington built by Mason between 1842-49. Masons' final home.

According to the 1871 Census Mason lived at Norwood House with his housekeeper, Hannah Winwood aged 55, three other servants, a gardener, a coachman and their families. He was still shown as living there in the year of his death 1881, this time with his grand-niece Ann Amelia Griffiths, aged 26, his housekeeper and a large number of servants. In 1895 the Dominican Sisters moved from their building in Orphanage Road, now occupied by the Conservative Party, to Norwood House, and St. Agnes Convent was established on the site, and in 1909 they started a private school. It is now the site of St. Edmund Campion Roman Catholic School, fronting to the main Birmingham to Sutton Coldfield Road.

There were many efforts to give public recognition of Mason works, in the form of a knighthood, a portrait for the Art Gallery, photographs for publication and a statue, but Mason always appeared to be the reluctant recipient. It was thought by some, including children at the orphanage that Mason turned down a knighthood when it was first offered, with the comment, "What's in a name". Whether this was true or just part of the mythology which surrounded many rich and famous people cannot be ascertained. However, the honour was accepted, along with an element of mystery. A statement on the foundation of the orphanage had been sent to Mr. Gladstone (55) the Prime Minister, who received Queen Victoria's command to offer Mason a knighthood. But when the Letters Patent received the Great Seal on the 30 November, 1872, Queen Victoria gave special permission that the presentation at court, and the personal laying on of the sword by the Queen could be dispensed with, and so the honour was bestowed by the Lord Lieutenant of Warwickshire. The reason given was Mason's age 77, and his general indisposition, and yet he had always been described as hail and hearty, and equal in energy to much younger men. It had also been pointed out that since his illness in the 1840's he had remaind in excellent health.

The following notice appeared in the London Gazette of the 3 December, 1872.

Whitehall, November 30th 1872

The Queen has been pleased to direct Letters Patent to be passed under the Great Seal granting the dignity of a knight of the United Kingdom of Great Britain and Ireland unto Josiah Mason of Norwood House, Erdington near Birmingham in the county of Warwick Esq.

The above was evidence that Mason was successful as an entrepreneur and philanthropist, and that this was acknowledged by others. Even though as Holyoake stated, that when he approached the local Members of Parliament to support the recommendation of a knighthood, "George Dixon assented but John Bright saw objections, and asked whether I saw it a good principle that a man should be made a knight because he had given £200,000 to the town".

55. *Letter from Prime Minister Gladstone offering knighthood 1872.*

However, efforts had continued to give public recognition in the form of a portrait, and from the time the orphanage opened in 1868 Birmingham Town Council in accepting their part of the Trust, had wanted to place a statue of Mason in the Corporation Art Gallery. Designs were obtained from several sculptors, unfortunately only one was accepted by the Town Council and this was rejected by Mason. Because of these difficulties the project was abandoned, much to Mason's relief as he had only reluctantly accepted the honour. However, many people still felt that his generosity should be recognised, and a public meeting was called and a private subscription list opened to pay for the painting of a portrait. Then a committee was formed which approached Mason for permission to proceed, when this was given, it was decided that the commission should go to Henry Turner Munns a members of The Royal Birmingham Society of Arts. For effect Munns chose to paint Mason in his own library, at Norwood House. He decided to paint a full length portrait on a canvas nine feet by six feet. (56) Mason was shown standing holding a pen in his right hand and an orphanage admission form, or cheque book in his left, ready to hand it to someone, to show his generosity. The portrait was said to be a good likeness, showing his high forehead, kindly eyes, white hair and beard, with clear fresh tints and lines, a clear physical image and a projection of his inner feelings.

Attention was given to detail, with a stick of red sealing wax on the pen tray of the library table, the pale green leather of the writing flap, a pad of pale green blotting paper tend to light up the sombre hue of the portrait.

56. *Full length portrait of Sir Josiah Mason by Henry Turner Munns, 1872.*

The general verdict of art critics and the public at the time was that it was admirable and an artistic likeness. It was finished in 1872 and presented to the Town Council in 1874 by Ralph Heaton, and placed in the Art Gallery which at the time was at Aston Hall. It is now on loan from the City Museum and Art Gallery to the University of Birmingham and hangs behind the chairman's seat in the Senate Room. Later a half length replica portrait by Mr. Munns was purchased by Mason's executors and placed in the board rooms of the college, and is still in the university's possession.

The following letter (57) also illustrates something of his reluctance, and concern against being exploited, or misrepresented in public.

> *Erdington, Birmingham*
> *January 6 1880*

Dear Sir,

If Guy Roslyn as(sic) applied(sic) to you for a negative of me don't trust him or help him in any way respecting my photo.

It may be for the new monthly the one I shew you.

> *Faithfully yours*
> *Josiah Mason*

Mr. H. Penn

Mason's resistance to be immortalised in the form of a statue met with little success, as a number were produced. There was mention of one, in the reminiscences of the orphanage's former residents. She recalls it standing in the corridor of the orphanage with the words, "A father to the fatherless, and the cause be knew not he searched out", inscribed above it. There were also a pair of alabaster busts of Mason and his wife in existence, which according to the Mason College Centenary Exhibition catalogue 1975, were made during their visit to Italy in 1848. None of these were on permanent display, until, following his death in 1881, the then Mayor of Birmingham called a meeting to raise funds for the erection of a public statue. Through the generosity of public subscriptions, the marble statue by the sculptor F.G. Williamson, was unveiled in 1885. It showed Mason in a comfortable pose seated with his back to Mason's College, holding the college foundation deed in his hand. It was placed in Edmund Street by the steps leading up from Ratcliffe Place, where it remained for 65 years. But damage, erosion by the weather and small acts of vandalism, such as on one occasion, in 1915, when Sir Oliver Lodge sent a porter to, "Remove at once the small boy sitting on Sir Josiah's knee" - all took their toll.

57. Hand written letter by Mason to H. Penn, photographer, 1880.

The statue was removed prior to the reconstruction work of 1951-52. Then for over a year the Erdington Historical Society in conjunction with the Birmingham Civic Society negotiated to have the statue re-erected near the orphanage he had built in Erdington. Subsequently the Public Works Committee decided to have it remodelled in the form of a bronze bust on an 8 foot stone pedestal, and inscribed, "Sir Josiah Mason". (58) The erosion damage was repaired by the sculptor William Bloye, and then forwarded to Messrs. Morris Singer Ltd., London for a bronze cast to be made. The pedestal of artificial stone with a gypsum finish was made by Messrs. Tarmac Ltd. Optimistically the Public Works Department hoped to have it on the traffic island at the junction of Orphanage Road and Chester Road, Erdington before the end of March 1953, but following the trial erection in February 1953, it had to be taken down for minor alterations.

58. Statue of Mason, Chester Road/Orphanage Road roundabout, Erdington. Erected 1963.

Members of the Erdington Historical Society were keen for an official unveiling ceremony, with representatives from Birmingham and Kidderminster. This was agreed and the unveiling was performed by the then Lord Mayor of Birmingham, Alderman P.W. Cox, J.P., who made a speech outlining the life and achievements of Sir Josiah Mason. The statue was placed facing the orphanage, a fact later commented on, as a suitable vantage point, for him to witness, in 1964, the demolition of his grand building.

The question still remains, as to whether Mason was happy with such public acclaim, or had wished to remain more enigmatically private. He never appeared to seek publicity or retain a high profile, but much of his life and work ensured that he gained both, and in the event he did not withdraw from either. It is clear that he had connections with people of high status and influence through whom he could express his wishes and exert his influence. It is known, that figures who loom large in a town's life can exert an influence without expressing it openly. But this latent political power is difficult to detect, and especially so in the case of Mason.

He did not conform to the notion that there is a close correlation between social, political and economic leadership, since he appeared not to exert power through the political system. Although by definition he was part of the local leadership, exerting influence by institutional means through his business and charitable enterprises, and also individually as an important part of the franchise, no evidence could be found of him exerting direct influence over local political decision making. That was apart from the fact that he was keen to transfer control of his orphanage and college to the Town Council, through the appointment of councillors as trustees after his death. But the fact that his indirect power and influence could not be detected, may have been the secret of his success.

Chapter 11
Conclusions

Mason's achievements can be measured in terms of his great personal wealth, and whether with altruistic intent or not, he also made a large and important contribution to Birmingham life. This was not only through the Victorian flair for grand architecture, and philanthropy, but by providing lasting opportunities for Birmingham people. This included the provision of a large orphanage and the establishment of non-sectarian education, which through his science college led to the establishment of Birmingham University. But additionally, although perhaps not intentionally he created increased opportunities for the employment of women. His entrepreneurial skills were also applied to assist Alexander Parkes, the Elkingtons, Krupps and Siemens to perfect their various inventions which included methods of water proofing, metal refining and plating. The results of which benefitted not only the country but probably the world.

To grasp what all this meant in the currency of the time, and the reasons for some incredulity, was as Skipp reminds us the fact that Mason's total philanthropy, must have been in excess of the produce of four years municipal rates. All the more incredible when compared with Joseph Gillott, another Birmingham penmaker and contemporary of Mason's who although a millionaire, and a great patron of arts, whose pictures realised £170,000 at his death, bequeathed a mere £3,000 to local charities.

There is every indication that Mason's philanthropy was approached in a similar way to his business, with Mason as the successful production engineer, boosted by his strong entrepreneurial, and organisational skills. This hypothesis is also extended to other aspects of his life particularly health and religion, which were approached in a technological way. He was a firm believer in homeopathic medicine, applying the illness to cure itself. His religious views bore some of the hallmarks of someone searching for diverse parts, bringing them together in a new, eclectic, non-sectarian form, and so provided a more balanced and personal way of looking at his faith.

He lived a healthy, well regulated frugal existence, rose early, walked a few miles before breakfast, ate plain food, drank a little wine but no spirits and had never smoked. It pleased him to set people a good example. An interesting anecdote told by Johnson illustrates how he was seen as niggardly in small things but open handed and very generous in large matters. The story goes that Mason upbraided Johnson for paying a 1/- for a cab fare and asked why he did not walk, Johnson indicated that had he done so he would have missed a £50 appointment.

His need to set a good example, and pay attention to detail also extended to the workplace where he had a great deal of personal contact with his workers, and with his phenomenal memory remembered all their names. Despite this he was said to have kept a dignified distance from them. However, Bunce recalls that he was not a dull man but recounts - in rather an overstated way - that he was cheerful, even tempered, serene, calm and kindly, and that his "moderate temperament did not exclude loveable qualities", quick to remember and show affection to relatives and old friends.

Although his illnesses may have been stress related, he appeared to have had interests which allowed him to relax. These included his interest in gardening which allowed him to indulge his love of flowers, and also extended to the way he enjoyed and collected works of art. According to a relative his favourite quotation, from Confucius, was, "Under all circumstances keep a quite mind".

Mason had two different sides to his character, the business and the benevolent, which in practice he kept separate. He enjoyed the cut and thrust of business, always appreciated a bargain, entered into negotiations with enthusiasm and was keen to achieve profits. The two sides of his personality were illustrated by two portraits which hung in his study at Norwood House. One showed him as sweet, paternal and affectionate and the other as severe, resolute and with what Mason called his business mouth. These descriptions seem to accord with the views of the people around him who thought him venerable, tenacious and resolute, and with biographical assessments peppered with positive attributes such as perceptive, reflective, intelligent and of kindly humour. His physical features also allowed for such descriptions with a broad high forehead, deep deep set eyes, prominent eyebrown and strong firm mouth coupled with long, soft white hair and beard.

A lighter comment on his wisdom and generosity from the rather biased pen of Beale. It appears that Mason often asked him to translate letters he received from abroad. One particular letter from an Italian Military Officer enclosed a photograph of his daughter, who by his account was not very attractive. The letter couched in rather flowery language, and full of flattery of Mason, indicated that her only hope of marriage was the receipt of a gift of £2,000 from Mason. A bill was presented for this amount which Mason promptly returned unpaid.

The views reflected above give some insight into Mason's personality, complicated and obscured as it was by the views of those who flattered, and those who wished to highlight his preceived meanness. Yet in the context of wealthy and successful men these personal characteristics were not untypical. What made him outstanding was the magnitude of his philanthropy, the extent of his industrial empire and his strong adherence to the principle of non-sectarian education. He would probably have succeeded during any period of history, but the Nineteenth Century allowed his talents to blossom undiminished.

59. Annie Mason, Sir Josiah's wife.

But one aspect of his life difficult to unravel, was the relationship with his wife, Annie, (59) and the contribution she made to his success. There are brief glimpses of her assisting him in the business in the early days at Lancaster Street, and other references to her during periods of crisis. She was with him on the "grand tour", she persuaded him to move out of town to Edgbaston, and was referred to in events at Norwood House. It was known from one account, that Mason was in the habit of addressing her affectionately as "Tet", and that they first set up home together in one of a row of tiny cottages opposite the glassworks in Bagot Street, where he worked. She was said to share his virtues of industry and frugality. He was distraught when she died on the 24 February, 1870, aged 78, after 52 years of marriage. She was buried in a vault in the orphanage grounds, at Erdington, over which in 1870 he built a mausoleum. (60) A fact commemorated on a embroidered plaque as Mason's Court, Olton.

60. *Mausoleum in the orphanage grounds Erdington where Josiah and Annie Mason were originally buried.*

The west window, of the mauseoleum, bore an inscription to his wife Annie, part of which said, "She rejoiced in all his efforts to do deeds of love". Inscriptions on other windows gave indications of Mason's character: the east window was said to have reminded the visitor, as the morning sun streamed through its coloured panes, of men who ministered to the needs of the helpless and the weak, "I am the good shepherd, and know my sheep, and am known of mine". The one on the north side had an inscription addressed to the trustees:-

They will be what you make them,
Make them wise and make them good,
Make them strong for time of trial;
Teach them temperance, self denial,
Patience, kindness, fortitude.

The remaining window on the west side had the inscription, "Suffer the little children to come unto me, and forbid them not: for of such is the kingdom of heaven". And underneath, "Whosoever shall give to drink unto one of these little ones a cup of cold water, shall in no wise lose his reward". The mausoleum had within its entrance, a statue of Mason.

On the 23 February, 1881, his 68th birthday, Mason held a dinner party at Norwood House, to which he invited the professors of the college, and the trustees of his other foundations. It was obvious to those present that he was unwell, and had difficulties with his sight and hearing, and although his mind was clear, he had difficulty in understanding what was going on around him. As the year progressed his health deteriorated. Firstly he developed a cold, and then on the 11 March after getting out of his customary vapour bath and walking a little way he missed his footing and had a fall which proved debilitating. This was a shock to his nervous system, revived an old retention of urine complaint and confined him to the house. As his condition deteriorated he remained in his room, and later took to his bed. It was apparent to those around him that he was very ill, although in no obvious pain. His doctors, Gibbs Blake and his assistant Huxley, were with him day and night for several weeks. It was still felt by those around him that he would recover, altough he did not share their optimism. Since the opening of the college on Thursday 1 October, 1880, he had been telling close friends that, "his work was done", and people noticed that he declined physically from that time.

Although aware of his approaching death he was described as cheerful and composed, he found prolonged conversation tiring, although he was alert and still able to recognize his family and friends. On Saturday, 11 June he said "Goodbye" to his friend and legal adviser Johnson, and then declined into a deep sleep. No further change was observed in his condition until 11am on 16 June when death was thought imminent. A further change in his breathing took place at 5pm, when it became very shallow. He died peacefully at 8pm. His great-nephew, Martyn Josiah Smith and housekeeper, Miss Winwood, were in the room at the time. His death was said to be due to old age. The casue of death certified on the Death Certificate by Dr. J. Gibbs Blake was "senile decay".

There were many expressions of sorrow when news of Mason's death became widely known particularly from the establishments he had built and developed. The staff and children at the orphanage, although they had been aware of his illness, were particularly stunned. Mason had made precise and detailed arrangements for his funeral, and stressed particularly, that it should be private and simple. Other instructions were that the coffin should be carried by six or eight of his old workmen or servants. His wishes were carried out on Saturday, 25 June, 1881 and the procession which left Norwood House consisted of eight bearers, followed by Dr. Gibbs Blake, Dr. J.C. Huxley, other mourners including G.J. Johnson, Martyn J. Smith, the Mayor of Birmingham (Alderman R. Chamberlain), Alderman Avery, R.L. Chance, J.T. Bunce, Dr. Heslop, G. Hookman, F. Holliday, J. Player and W. Rogers, trustees respectively of the college and orphanage, F. Elkington, J.B. Braithwaite (London), J.F. Stewart (Dundee), C.A. Harrison, E.D. Robinson, S. Jevons, J.B. Matthews and W. Hodgkiss. They walked through the grounds to a small gate, then along Bell Lane to the orphanage. Bell Lane was crowded with vehicles and people, who had to peer over the hedge to see the ceremony.

A solemn and hushed service was held in the Orphanage Chapel. Then 150 boys and 200 girls dressed in their Inverness capes, because it was a miserable wet day, walked to the mausoleum in the orphanage grounds. Mason's wife Annie had been buried there in 1870. At the entrance to the vault were Professors Tilden, Bridge, Poynting and Arber of the Science College, L. Allport, the curator and librarian, G.H. Morley, secretary, W. Bach, trustee of the orphanage, Rev. B. Wright, M. Pollack, S.F. Rollason, W.E. Wiley, J.H. Barclay, W. Clements, and a number of students from the college, and officials from the orphanage. The service was conducted by the Rev. Hyla H. Rose, Vicar of Erdington, and in line with Mason's views was an abridgement of the Church of England burial service. The children stood with the others around the railing of the mausoleum and sang, "Beloved and Honoured Fare Thee Well", this had been written by their head teacher, J.T. Read and set to music by A. Tubb the music teacher. Many of the children became very upset at this point.

The coffin, made of polished oak and brass fittings had a plate with the inscription, "Sir Josiah Mason, Knight, Born 23rd February 1795, died 16th June 1881", was lowered into the vault. Following the benediction and the end of the service a number of people went down into the vault. Among them were six representatives of the children with two weaths to place on the coffin. According to an account by one of them, as they descended they saw Mason's wife's coffin with a faded wreath. Then one unfortunate boy assuming that the steps led all the way down, realised too late that there were only six or seven, fell sprawling across the coffin. In his shocked and frightened state he scrambled out, but was most concerned about having spoiled his new suit.

Mason may have thought that his request for a private and simple service had been disregarded as it turned out to be such a large event. Although an item in the Daily Post of Monday, 27 June, indicated that many people in Birmingham would have wished to honour him with a much more public funeral.

The burial was duly entered in the Erdington Parish Registers as follows:- 1881 Josiah Mason Knt. Norwood House, Erdington, June 25 Aged 86 Hyla H. Rose, Vicar. A mourning card was issued which read:

In affectionate memory of:

SIR JOSIAH MASON, Knight
Founder of The Orphanage and
Almshouses at Erdington
The Mason Science College, Birmingham
Born at Kidderminster, February 23rd 1795
Died at Erdington, June 16th 1881

"I delivered the poor that cried, and the fatherless and him that had none to help him". JOB XX1X 12

"By the blessing of the Lord, I profited and filled my wine press like a gatherer of grapes. Consider that I laboured not for myself only but for all them that seek learning". ECCLESIASTICS XXXIII.

Other cards were also issued written by M. Matthews, addressed to My Dear Children and On The Death of Sir Josiah Mason. They outlined his great works, compassion and rewards that had accumulated for him in heaven.

Mason's Will (see appendix 2) produced some interesting insights into his family life. This was one of the few pieces of evidence to place him within a family, as against his business and philanthropic interests. References to his and his wife's family, show that contact was maintained over a period of years, although little mention was made of them in the available literature or correspondence.

Martyn Josiah Smith son of his nephew Isaac Smith was very involved with Mason's business. Mason's clear aspirations for his great nephew are detailed in the generous bequests made under the Will, and as one of the co-executors he was given considerable authority to manage large parts of the estate. However, Mason's plan was for his great nephew to take over his nickel refining interests.

The Will was extensive, and servants were not forgotten, Hannah Winwood his housekeeper, and the former matrons of the orphanage Ann and Caroline Stockwin were given annuities and the use for life of property in South Grove, Erdington. His Will outlined in detail the steps to be taken to protect his money against all contingencies. This ensured that people were able to gain the maximum benefit from their inheritance. Clauses ensured the most beneficial investment of monies, as though in death he wished to continue the thrifty habits of a lifetime. This record of bequests to family members allowed a short family tree to be drawn up, other detail being added from research findings. (see appendix 1)

For all his meticulous planning and attention to detail during his lifetime arranging his funeral, Will and burial in the mausoleum, he could never have predicted the events 80 years later, when in January 1964, the mausoleum in the orphanage grounds was taken down to provide room for extensions to Yenton Primary School.

Prior to that an application had been made to the Home Office for the removal of bodies from the site. On the 25 September, 1961, this permission was granted with a "Notice of Intended Removal of Human Remains and Monuments or Tombstones from the Burial Ground (61) and Mausoleum at Sir Josiah Mason's Orphanage Erdington". The list of names in the "Notice", included Mason, his wife Annie and 54 orphanage children. They were all cremated at Perry Barr crematorium in 1961. A plaque (62) in a walled area of the crematorium, aptly named Mason Court, stands high on the wall opposite the entrance, and contains all their names. It stands proud of its surroundings, is marble coloured with the names etched in red. The walled garden is well maintained, planted with lawn, flowers and rose bushes. Recently the Sir Josiah Mason Trust have arranged for it to be cleaned. It is a peaceful and pleasant place for Mason's ashes to be among those of the children he endeavoured to help so much.

61. Childrens' burial place in orphanage grounds, Erdington.

THE REMAINS OF SIR JOSIAH MASON & HIS WIFE ANNIE
TOGETHER WITH THE FOLLOWING ORPHAN CHILDREN
WERE REMOVED FROM THE GROUNDS OF THE SIR JOSIAH
MASONS ORPHANAGE AND CREMATED HERE IN 1962
A·E·MATTHEWS A·G·SMITH M·A·HUGHES H·CLIFF L·MORRIS
E·M·SEXSMITH E·KING A·M·SWIFT S·MABBETT M·KIRKHAM
A·JAMES R·A·HAND A·WHEELER S·A·DAY M·WHITEHOUSE
J·E·NOLAN E·S·KING F·DILLON L·E·HOTCHKISS H·M·MILLS
L·NEWEY J·E·PRATT J·E·PRESTON E·COTTERILL J·GASKIN
C·TAYLOR L·MORGAN E·HOWSHIP R·VINTON M·HOMER
E·COOKE F·K·WINDSOR C·SMITH F·H·ALLSOP M·E·PURVER
C·E·LEWIS M·A·FRENCH L·GIBSON G·BASSETT G·BURNS
M·A·HAYNES R·M·DIXON A·H·BOWERS S·LAIGHT W·J·LANE
G·E·ALLWOOD F·WHEELER H·COLLINS F·E·LANE F·SPRATT
A·PHILLIPS H·D·BARNES C·TANNER C·COSSAGE

62. *Plaque at Perry Barr Crematorium where ashes of Josiah and Annie Mason with 54 orphanage children re-interred in 1962.*

Appendix 1

FAMILY TREE

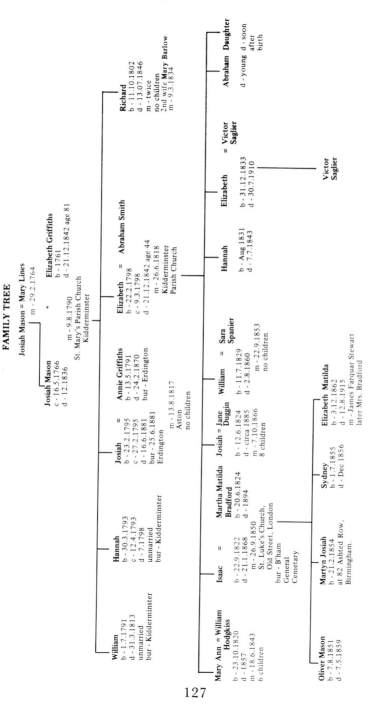

Josiah Mason = Mary Lines
m - 29.2.1764

Josiah Mason = Elizabeth Griffiths
c - 16.5.1766   b - 1761
d - 12.1836   d - 21.12.1842 age 81
m - 9.8.1790
St. Mary's Parish Church
Kidderminster

William
b - 1.7.1791
d - 31.3.1813
unmarried
bur - Kidderminster

Hannah
b - 30.3.1793
c - 12.4.1793
d - 7.1798
unmarried
bur - Kidderminster

Josiah = Annie Griffiths
b - 23.2.1795   b - 13.5.1791
c - 27.2.1795   d - 24.2.1870
d - 16.6.1881   bur - Erdington
bur - 25.6.1881
Erdington

m - 13.8.1817
Aston
no children

Elizabeth = Abraham Smith
b - 22.2.1798
c - 9.3.1798
d - 21.12.1842 age 44
m - 26.6.1818
Kidderminster
Parish Church

Richard
b - 11.10.1802
d - 13.07.1846
m - twice
no children
2nd wife Mary Barlow
m - 9.3.1834

Mary Ann = William Hodgkiss
b - 23.10.1820
d - 1857
m - 18.6.1843
6 children

Isaac = Martha Matilda Bradford
b - 22.9.1822   b - 20.6.1824
d - 21.11.1868   d - 1894
m - 26.9.1850
St. Luke's Church,
Old Street, London
bur - B'ham
General
Cemetary

Josiah = Jane Duggin
b - 12.6.1824
d - circa 1885
m - 7.10.1866
8 children

William = Sara Spanier
b - 11.7.1829
d - 2.8.1860
m - 22.9.1853
no children

Hannah
b - Aug 1831
d - 7.7.1843

Elizabeth = Victor Saglier
b - 31.12.1833
d - 30.7.1910

Abraham Daughter
d - young   d - soon
after
birth

Oliver Mason
b - 7.8.1851
d - 7.5.1859

Sydney
b - 1.7.1855
d - Dec 1856

Martyn Josiah
b - 21.2.1854
at 82 Ashted Row,
Birmingham.

Elizabeth Matilda
b - 3.12.1862
d - 12.8.1915
m - James Farquar Stewart
later Mrs. Bradford

Victor Saglier

Appendix 2

Notes of Will:

Will proved 29th August 1881
Gross value of Estate £56,727.5.7
Johnson, Barclay and Johnson Solicitors, Birmingham.

1. Will drawn up 1st June 1878

2. Appointment of Trustees:

    My friend George James Johnson, solicitor Birmingham and great nephew Martyn Josiah Smith (son of my late nephew Isaac Smith) to be executors and trustees.

3. Bequest of Annuities:

    a   Victor Saglier the younger, husband of my niece Elizabeth an annuity of £80 for life and then to his wife, if she survives him, for her life.
    b   Sara widow of my late nephew William Smith £52 annuity, during her life.
    c   Niece Ann Hodgkiss £52 annuity for life and then for her husband if he survives her.
    d   Housekeeper Hannah Winwood £100 annuity for life.
    e   Ann Stockwin now of the Orphanage, Erdington £70, annuity for life and to her sister Caroline the same.

    All free of legacy tax, to be paid quarterly from the date of my death. The first payment to be three calendar months after my decease.

4. Pecuniary Legacies:

    To be paid in addition to any annuities due, and free of legacy tax.
    a   Son of Victor Saglier the younger, £500 at age 21.
    b   Mademoiselle Isabella Saglier sister of Victor £100.
    c   Each of the children of my niece Ann Hodgkiss £100 at age 21.
    d   Each of the children of my nephew Josiah Smith £100 at age 21.

e To great niece Elizabeth Matilda Stewart daughter of my late nephew Isaac Smith £1,200 minus any advances to her or her husband, £500 already settled on her and £300 formerly given makes £2,000.

f To Mary Taplin now of Melbourne Australia relative of my late wife £200.

g To Ann Griffiths daughter of Richard Griffiths another relative of my late wife proceeds of a £1000 policy no. 9438 Scottish National Insurance Company on the life of Thomas Allock purchased through bankruptcy. Trustees to keep up payments. To receive 10/- (50p) per week until policy payable.

h George James Johnson for looking after my affairs £1,000.

i Martyn Josiah Smith great nephew - on condition of winding up Nickel business, incase he shall not purchase same as here provided £10,000.

5. Bequest of Use of Houses South Grove

Hannah Winwood use for personal occupation 1 of messages (house) South Grove, Erdington. Ann and Caroline Stockwin the same. Repairs of outside to be met from the estate.

6. £3,000 to Trustees to fulfil Testators Directions

To be free of legacy duty on trust. For secret memorials and other minor matters to be kept secret until my death. Any money left after actions of the memorandum to be part of estate of residuary legatee.

7. Special Charge of Legacies First on Real Estate and Then on Impure Personality

Real estate to be primary fund in discharge of all my personal estate. When that exhausted then portion of personal estate not by law capable of been given to charity. To pay all funeral, testamentary expenses, debts pecuniary legacies, annuities and all legacy duty.

8. General Devise and Bequest to Trustees

Conversion of all personal and real estate to money by sale or otherwise, adhering to Statute 23 and 24 year of the reign of her present majesty Chapter 145.

9. Special Clause as to Business

Before proceeding to sell my business of a nickel manufacture, Trustees shall deal in the following manner:

a   Within six calendar months Martyn Josiah Smith shall decide and agree with Trustees or Executors whether he wishes to purchase the business including land and buildings at Briches Green where the business is carried on.

b   If Martyn Josiah Smith decides to purchase he shall agree with the other Trustees or Executors how to pay by instalments or in some other manner.

c   If Martyn Josiah Smith does not purchase or lease, the Trustees or Executors shall not consent to the terms of payment. The business should be sold as a going concern or wound up by agreement of Trustee or Executor.

d   During the time allowed by Martyn Josiah Smith to decide or that it takes to wind up or dispose of the business, the following action should be taken:

1   To employ all capital in the business and other portions of my personal or real estate for the business

2   To employ the Manager, or Manager Clerk, servants, workmen, workwomen and pay such salary or wages or money or interest in proportions of profits or in lieu or additional to salary or wages. Martyn Josiah Smith to receive the same salary that he is in receipt of at the time of my death.

3   To purchase take or lease, or other wise acquire land and buildings the Trustees need to continue the business.

4   Trustees can operate business as if their own without fear of liability for any loss etc.

10. Sale and Conversion May by Postponed - Special Directions as to Shares

Permission to postpone sale of any real or personal estate to obtain best payment - enhance debentures and shares in various joint stock companies which had to be sold in twelve months after my death. They can be retained to obtain best value for the estate.

11. Application of Trusts of Proceeds of Real and Personal Estate

Trustees can pay debts, funeral expenses, annuities, legacies etc. by:

a   Selling debentures in Perry & Co. Ltd. absolved against loss
     of pure or impure personality (amount of personal estate
     available by law for charitable purposes or not available).
b   Investing for annuities in H.M. Government or Public Com-
     pany in Great Britain.

12. Special Provisions as to Marshalling Assets for Charitable
    Purposes
    Referred to as pure personality (amount of personal estate avail-
    able by law for charitable purposes) or not available impure per-
    sonality. The primary source of payment of debts, legacies, ann-
    uities and other expenses shall be my real estate, then my im-
    pure personality but only at the discretion of the Executors and
    as a last resort.

13. Direction as to Surplus of Pure Personalty
    To be used for the completion of buildings in course of erection
    by me on land subject to trusts of certain debenture dated 12th
    December 1870 between me and James Gibbs Blake and George
    James Johnson being the Deed of Foundation intended to be
    called Josiah Mason's Scientific College or Josiah Mason College
    for the study of Practical Science for equipment, professor-
    ships, scholarships, exhibitions and prizes.

14. Investment Clause
    Trustees have the power to invest any money not immediately
    needed.

15. Power to Compromise Actions, Suits etc
    Power of Executors to take any necessary legal actions etc., in
    connection with the will.

16. Special Clauses as to the Remuneration of Trustees for Prof-
    essional Services
    G.J. Johnson to remain as solicitor and to charge fees for work
    on the estate in addition to his legacy, trustees allowance, etc.

17. Trustees Indemnity Clause
    Trustees only responsible for own defaults or misappropriation.

18. Delcaration as to Acts 23rd and 24th Victoria Chapter 145
    Will subject to but not constrained by the above legislation.

In witness there of .... my last will etc. (on 13 sheets of paper .... on 13th sheet set my hand....

Josiah Mason

J.H. Barclay, Solicitor, Birmingham
W. Showell Rogers, Clerk to Messrs. Johnson,
Barclay and Johnson

Codicil

1. Codicil made 8th January 1881 to Will of 1st June 1878.
2. Whereas I have this day transferred to my great nephew Martyn Josiah Smith securities of £10,000 and all my benefit in the land and buildings at Birches Green in the 9th clause of my will. I now revoke the legacy to him of £10,000 under the 4th clause of my will.
3. Whereas I am desirous to facilitate the acquistion by my great nephew Martyn Josiah Smith of my business of nickel manufacture, I increase the power of the other executor under clause 9.
4. The purhcase of the business can be by instalments over 7 years without security.
5. Other Trustee to assess value of nickel business.
6. Power to G.J. Johnson to continue, sell or wind up the nickel business as he thinks fit.

Signed Josiah Mason,

Witness William Johnson Solicitor, Birmingham
J.H. Barclay, Solicitor, Birmingham

Proved with a codicil at Birmintham 29th August 1881.

132

Appendix 3

MASON'S FRIENDS AND ASSOCIATES BY OCCUPATION, POLITICS, RELIGION AND MEMBERSHIP OF BIRMINGHAM ORGANISATIONS

NAME:	OCCUPATION:	POLITICS:	RELIGION:	Direct Involvement with Mason			Membership of other Birmingham Organisations							
				College Trustees	Orphanage Trustees	Partner/Associates	Hospitals	Town Council	Library Committees	Edgbaston Debating Society	King Edward School	Birmingham and Midland Institute	Charities	Justice of the Peace
W.C. Aitken	Manager of Metal Works	Liberal	N.K.	*					*			*		
Thomas Avery	Manufacturer	Liberal	N.K.	*				*m						
Samuel Beale	Banker M.P.	N.K.	N.K.					*m						
Dr. Gibbs Blake	Doctor	N.K.	N.K.	*	*		*h							
John Thackeray Bunce	Newspaper Editor	Liberal	C of E	*					*	*				*
Dr Thomas Poetius Heslop	Doctor Prof. of Physics	Liberal	N.K.	*			*ch				*			
Frank Holliday	N.K.	N.K.	N.K.		*			*						
George Hookman	N.K.	Liberal	N.K.	*										*
Solomon Jevons	N.K.	N.K.	Meth.		*								*nch	
George Holyoake	Foundary Worker	Co-op	Atheist		*									
G.J. Johnson	Prof. of Law Queen's College	Liberal	Non-C	*	*	*	*q	*m	*	*	*			*
George Player	Button Manufacturer	Liberal	Baptist		*								*	

NAME:	OCCUPATION:	POLITICS	RELIGION:	Direct Involvement with Mason			Membership of other Birmingham Organisations							
				College Trustees	Orphanage Trustees	Partner/Associates	Hospitals	Town Council	Library Committees	Edgbaston Debating Society	King Edward School	Birmingham and Midland Institute	Charities	Justice of the Peace
Maurice Pollack	Director Pen Company	Liberal	N.K.			*p		*m				*	*	*
William Rogers	Builder	Liberal	Baptist		*		*w	*	*				*	
George Shaw	Patent Agent Prof. Chemistry Queen's College	None	N.K.	*								*_		
Martyn Josiah Smith	N.K.	N.K.	N.K.	*	*									
William Wiley	Manager Pen Factory	N.K.	N.K.			*p								
L.H. Elkington	Manufacturer Electro-Plating	Con	C of E			*p	*q						*	
P.H. Muntz	N.K.	Liberal M.P.	N.K.				*m							
W. Fothergill Batho	Engineer Manager of Pen works	N.K.	N.K.			*p								
R.L. Chance (Jun)	N.K.	N.K.	N.K.				*h							
Isaac Horton	Pork Butcher/ Property Developer	N.K.	N.K.	*	*	*							*	
Alexander Parkes	Chemist/ Inventor	N.K.	N.K.			*								

NOTE: N.K. = not known, M = Mayor, P = Partner,
HOSPITALS: H = Homeopathic, CH = Childrens, Q = Queens
METH = Wesleyan Methodist, CofE = Church of England
NON-C = Non Conformist Church of the Saviour
CON = Conservative

SOURCE: Compiled from Birmingham Reference Library, History and Geography Department copies of Biography and Review, Edgbastonia, Newspaper Cuttings, Birmingham Biography, Birmingham Worthies in Birmingham Weekly Post, Birmingham Gazette, Birmingham Daily Post, Familiar Figures from Evening Despatch.

Bibliography

PRIMARY SOURCES

Unpublished

1. Birmingham Reference Library (Hereafter BRL), History and Geography Department, R.S. Leader, History of Elkington & Co., typescript, 53pp, C1913.

2. BRL, History and Geography Department, Patent Index, (Birmingham Industries) compiled by Barbara Smith, Birmingham University, (uncatalogued) Perry & Co. Ltd., Acc 325260, Orphanage Deed 41.3, Acc 31068, Foundation Deed of Mason's Science College, L.48.1, 1880. Aston, Erdington, Census 171.

3. BRL, Archives Division, Josiah Mason (1795-1881), MS 1609, Letter William Jeff Deed 572 475, (DV 830), MS 1691, MS 1332/85 18 Dec 1872, Methodist Records, M.B. 2/4, MS 1631 Orphanage Foundation Deed, 41.3 Acc 31068, Josiah Mason's Orphanage MS 1631, Parish Registers, Aston, Great Levy Book.

4. Birmingham University Collection, 7/IV/7/39, 4/II/7, 4/IV/7/3, L add 5239.

5. British Library Newspaper Library, London, B1163, Iron-monger, 1864-1871.

6. Erdington Historical Society Transactions, 1952, 1953, Tithe Apportionment, 1845.

7. Kidderminster, Parish Registers, St. Mary & All Saints Church.

8. Manchester City Library, Local Studies, Renold Archive Perry & Co.

9. PRO BT31/2185, Perry & Co. Ltd., Company number 10224.

10. PRO BT31/3873 Elkington & Co. Ltd., Company number 24440.

11. Somerset House, Will of Sir Josiah Mason, 1 June 1881.

12. Victoria & Albert Museum, Archives, Elkington & Co., Vol 2, Add 3, 1979, PL1, Vol 3.

Published

Official

1. **Birmingham Council Minutes,** Foundation Deed of Orphanage, 3 August 1869. Trustees of Science College, 5 July 1881.

2. Birmingham Council, **Abstract of Statistics,** 1831-1954,1956.

3. Birmingham Education Committee, Juvenile Employment and Welfare Sub-Committee. **Report of Conditions of Employment of Juveniles in Birmingham Trades - Jewellery, Silver and Electro-Plate Trades,** January 1926.

4. **Childrens Employment (Trades and Manufacturers)** PP 1843, XIV.

5. **Childrens Employment,** PP 1864, XIV.

6. **Factories, Half Yearly Reports by Inspectors of Factories made to the Government,** PP 1841 X.

7. **Institution of Mechanical Engineers Proceedings,** 1886.

8. London and North Western Railway, (Sutton Coldfield Branch), Act 1859, 22-23, Vic, CIXXXVII

9. **Royal Commission on Factory and Workshops Acts,** PP 1876 XXIX, CMD 1443.

Newspapers and Journals

1. **Birmingham Daily Gazette,** 24 February 1875, 6 May 1869.

2. **Birmingham Daily Post,** 4 August 1866, 24 March 1868, 3 March 1869, 16 November 1886, 2 August 1869, 4 December 1872, 30 December 1873, 24 February 1875, 2 October 1880, 17 June 1881, 27 June 1881, 9 July 1881, 4 August 1881, 1 September 1881.

3. **Birmingham Weekly News,** 22 March 1875.

4. Birmingham Weekly Post, 3 March 1950.

5. British Trades Journal, Industrial Celebrations, 1 May 1876.

6. Burdetts Official Intelligence, 1882.

7. The Engineer, 16 November 1877, June 1870.

8. Kidderminster Shuttle, 25 June 1881.

9. Mason's College Magazine, October 1885.

10. Illustrated Midland News, 1890.

11. Nature, 25 February 1875.

12. Sutton and Erdington Times, 5 September 1891.

13. The Times, 17 June 1881.

SECONDARY SOURCES

Books

1. G.C. Allen, The Industrial Development of Birmingham and the Black Country, 1860-1927, 1986.

2. J.H. Andrew, The Birmingham Pen Trade, 1981.

3. T.S. Ashton, The Industrial Revolution, 1760-1830, 1968.

4. W.W.M. Beale, The Light of Other Days, 1890.

5. D. Bebbington, Victorian Nonconformity, 1992.

6. C. Behagg, Politics and Production in the early Nineteenth Century, 1990.

7. G.P. Bevan, (Ed), The British Manufacturing Industries - the Birmingham Trades, III, 1876.

8. F. Boase, Modern English Biography, II, 1851-1900, 1906.

9. H. Bore, The Story of the Invention of Steel Pens, 1886.

10. I.C. Bradley, Enlightened Entrepreneurs, 1987.

11. A. Briggs, **History of Birmingham**, II, 1952.

12. J.T. Bunce, **Josiah Mason: a biography** (printed for private circulation), 1882.

13. J.T. Bunce, **Josiah Mason: a biography with sketches of the History of the Steel Pen and Electro-Plating Trades**, 1890.

14. F.W. Buntall & C.G. Burton, **Souvenir History of the Foundation and Development of the Mason Science College and the University of Birmingham**, 1930.

15. D. Cannadine, **Lords & Landlords; the Aristocracy and Towns 1774-1967**, 1980.

16. A.A.S. Charles, **The Steel Pen Trade, 1930-1980**, 1983.

17. M. Cheesewright, **Mirror to a Mermaid**, 1975.

18. R.V. Clements, **Local Notables and the City Council**, 1969.

19. F. Crouzet, **The First Industrialists**, 1985.

20. R.K. Dent, **Old and New Birmingham**, 111, 1973.

21. **Fortunes made in Business**, III, unattributed, 1884.

22. D. Fraser, **The Evolution of the British Welfare State**, 1984 (2nd Ed).

23. J.A. Garrard, **Leadership and Power in Victorian Industrial Towns, 1830-1880**, 1983.

24. C. Gill, **History of Birmingham**, Vol 1, 1952.

25. E.P. Hennock, The Social Composition of Borough Councils in two large cities, 1835-1914 in H.J. Dyos, Ed. **The Study of Urban History**, 1968.

26. G.J. Holyoake, **Sixty Years of an Agitators Life**, 1990.

27. E. Hopkins, **Birmingham: the First Manufacturing Town in the World, 1760-1840**, 1989.

28. T. Insull, **John Cadbury, 1801-1889**, 1979, (private circulation).

29. J.A. Langford, **Modern Birmingham and its Institutions**, 1871.

30. C. Lapworth, **The Mason College and Technical Education,** 1884.

31. R. Lea, **Steaming Up to Sutton,** 1984.

32. P.T. Marsh, **Josiah Chamberlain - Entrepreneur in Politics,** 1994.

33. H. McLachlan, **The Unitarian Movement in the Religious Life of England 1700-1900,** 1934.

34. D. Mole, Attitude of Churchmen towards Society in Early Victorian Birmingham in A. Bryman, Ed., **Religion in the Birmingham area: Essays in the Sociology of Religion,** 1975.

35. D.E. Owen, **English Philanthropy 1660-1960,** 1965.

36. P.L. Payne, **British Entrepreneurship in the Nineteenth Century,** 1974.

37. E.A. Pratt, **Successful Lives of Modern Times,** 1901.

38. W.D. Rubinstein, Men of Property: some aspects of occupation, inheritance and power among top British Wealtholders, in Philip Stanworth and Antony Giddens, **Elites and Power in British Society,** 1974.

39. M. Sanderson, **The Universities and British Industry 1850-1970,** 1972.

40. V. Skipp, **The making of Victorian Birmingham,** 1983.

41. S. Smiles, **Self Help,** 1875.

42. D. Smith, **Conflict and Compromise - class formation in English Society 1830-1914,** 1982.

43. M.D. Stephens and G.W. Roderick, (Eds), **Samuel Smiles and Nineteenth Century Self-Help in Education,** 1983.

44. S. Timmins, **The Birmingham and Midland Hardware District,** 1866.

45. L. Taylor, **The Study of Sir Josiah Mason the prince of pen-makers,** 1894.

46. T. Tholfsen, **Working Class radicalism in mid-Victorian England,** 1976.

47. D.M. Thompson, The Liberation Society 1844-1868 in Patricia Hollis, **Pressure from Without in Early Victorian England,** 1974.

48. J. Tompkinson, **Kidderminster,** 1953.

49. C. Upton, **A History of Birmingham,** 1993.

50. **Victorian County History,** VII, Warwickshire, Birmingham 1964

51. E.W. Vincent and P. Hinton, **The University of Birmingham its history and significance,** 1947.

52. K.Warren, **The British Iron and Steel Sheet Industry since 1840,** 1970.

53. G. Watson, **The English Ideology,** 1973.

54. M.R. Watts, **The Dissenters,** 1978.

55. I.L. Wedley, **Sir Josiah Mason his life and works,** 1928.

Articles

1. **Biograph and Review,** Sir Josiah Mason, P.H. Muntz, III, 1881.

2. **Dictionary of National Biography,** Alexander Parkes, III, 1974.

3. **Edgbastonia,** July 1881, July 1885.

4. B. Harrison, "Philanthropy and the Victorians" **Victorian Studies,** IX, 1966.

5. E.P. Hennock, "Finance and Politics in Urban Social Government in England 1835-1900', in **Historical Journal,** VI, 2, 1963.

6. D.J. Jeremy, "Josiah Mason" in D.J. Jeremy (Ed), **Dictionary of Business Biography,** IV, 1985.

7. D.J. Jeremy, Anatomy of the British Business Elite, 1860-1980, in **Business History,** XXV, 1983.

8. Linda J. Jones, "Public Pursuit of Private Profit? Liberal Business and Municipal Politics in Birmingham, 1865-1900", in **Business History,** XXV, 1983.

9. C. Penney, The Lion, The Book and the Mermaid, or How the University Got Its Arms in **Midland Ancestor,** 7, 12 June 1986.

10. W.D. Rubinstein, New Men of Wealth and the Purchase of Land in Nineteenth Century England, **Past and Present,** 92, 1981.

11. B.M.D. Smith, "Patents for Invention: the National and Local Picture, **Business History,** IV, 1962.

12. T.R. Tholfsen, The Artisan and the Culture of Early Victorian Birmingham, **Birmingham University Historical Journal,** IV, 2, 1954.

13. Charles Wilson, The Entrepreneur in the Industrial Revolution in Britain, **History,** XLII, 144, 1957.

14. D.L. Wykes, Religious Dissent and the Penal Laws: an explanation of business success, **History,** 75, 243, February 1990.

OTHER

Unpublished Thesis and Private Communications

1. M. Harrison, Social Reform in late Victorian and Edwardian Manchester with special reference to T.C. Horsfall, Manchester University, PhD Thesis, 1987.

2. N.C. Marston, Sir Josiah Mason's Contribution to Education in Birmingham, Open University Dissertation, 1980.

3. D.E.H. Mole, The Church of England and Society in Birmingham, 1830-1866, University of Cambridge, Phd Thesis, 1962.

4. F.L. Timmins, Birmingham Steel Pen Trade, after 1826, University of Birmingham, M. Comm Thesis, 1925.

5. Telephone conversation with a Mrs Devonald re a proposed adoption.

6. Telephone conversation with a Mr D. Nockold, descendant of Mason.

7. Conversations and practical assistance from Philip Poole, Pen Dealer, London.

8. Conversations with and written information from John A. Nicholson, Burry Port, Dyfed.

Index

AITKEN, William Costin 86
ALLEN, Frederick 68, 81
ALMSHOUSES 17, 56
AMERICA 43, 49
ARCHITECT 60, 61, 81, 86
ARGYLL, Duke of 69
ASTON, Parish Church 3
ASTON HALL 113
AVERY, Thomas 81, 87, 105

BACH, William 68
BAGOT STREET 3, 10, 12
BAKEWELL, Mrs 12, 56
BAKEWELL, Richard 10, 12
BALDWIN, Stanley 96
BAPTISTS 68
BAND OF HOPE 65
BATHO, William Fothergill 34, 68
BEALE 105
BEALE, Willert 1, 4, 56, 106, 118
BEAUMONT, William 100
BEAUMONT, J.A. 100
BEAUMONT, W.H. 99, 100
BEGGARS 21
BELL LANE 60, 65, 69, 79
BELMONT ROW CHAPEL 12, 14, 15
BEROL 43
BERWOOD HOUSE 107, 109
BICKENHILL 65
BIGGS 89
BINGLEY HOUSE 46
BIRMINGHAM 17, 25, 27, 40,
45, 49, 91
  Art Gallery 111
  Central Library 97
  Council Minutes 95
  Civic Society 97
  Education Department 69, 84
  Land 65
  Festival Choral Society 91
  Mayors 105
  Population 35
  Public Works Committee 113
  Queen's Hotel 92

  Royal Society of Arts 112
  Science Museum 46
  Town Council 65, 115
  Town Hall 76, 86
BIRMINGHAM & 33, 46, 86
  MIDLAND INSTITUTE
BIRMINGHAM BANKING CO. 42,
43, 98, 100
  Ceased Business 100
  Shareholders Meeting 100
BIRMINGHAM DAILY POST 92
BIRMINGHAM UNIVERSITY 96
  Clock Tower 96
  Grant of Arms 95
  Royal Charter 96
  Students Union 95
  Senate Room 113
BIRMINGHAM STREETS
  Bristol Road 107
  Cliveland Street 87
  Congreave Street 86
  Easy Row 102
  Edmund Street 86, 87
  Great Charles Street 12, 86, 87
  Lancaster Street 12, 13, 28, 33,
34, 40, 42, 43, 52, 71, 87, 120
  Paradise Street 86
  Princip Street 87
  Steelhouse Lane 87
BLACK COUNTRY 25
BLAKE, James Gibb 43, 68, 81, 86,
87, 103, 122
BLOYE, William 113
BORE, Henry 39
BOTHAM, J.R. 60, 61
BOTTOMLEY, Horatio William 17
69, 73, 74
BOULTON & WATT 45
BRACE FACTORY 55
BRAITHWAITE, J.B. 87
BREARLEY Street Works 48, 51
BRIGHT, John 106, 111
  Speech 89
BRITISH PENS 44

BROAD STREET 46
BULL STREET 27
BULLOCK, Edwin 102
BUNCE, John Thackray 1, 12, 32,
43, 48, 81, 86, 88, 91, 104, 107, 118
BURRY PORT 53
  Schools 53
BUSINESS 21, 24

CADBURY, George 107
CADBURY'S Rock Cocoa 80
CALTHORPE, Lord 96
CAMBRIDGE University 91
CARNEGIE 96
CATECHISM 19, 58, 79
CHAMBERLAIN, Joseph 89, 92,
95, 96
CHAMBERLAIN, Neville 96
CHAMBERLAIN, Richard 65, 91
  Mayor 65, 91
CHANCE, Robert Lucas 63, 81, 102
CHAPEL 14
CHAPLAIN 79
CHRISTIAN, Henry 102
CHURCH of England 15, 19
CIVIC Gospel 25
CO-OPERATIVE Movement 17
COOPER 81
COPPER Smelting 53
CONFUCIUS 118
CONGREGATIONALISTS 68
CONSTRUCTORS 55
COSSINS, Jethro A. 81, 86
COTTAGES, Bell Lane 69
COX, F.W. Alderman 115
CRIPPEN, Dr. 69
CROSSKEY, Rev 96
CUTLERY 48, 50

DAILY Post 92
DALE, R.W. 81
DAMMANN, Karl 96
DAVIS, W.T. 83
DELTA Metal Company 52
DILLON, Mr & Mrs 73
DIXON, A 102
DIXON, George 111
DOGS 81
DONKEY 8
DOWELL'S Retreat 69
DRANE, John 29
DUFRENE, M. Franconneau 23

EDGBASTON 96, 107
EDUCATION
  Liberal 85
  Literary 91
  Scientific 91
  University 91
ELECTRICITY 33, 92
ELECTRO-PLATING 26, 32, 34,
45, 49
  Government Report 1864 51
ELKINGTON & Co 26, 92
ELKINGTON, Henry 45, 51
ELKINGTON, Frederick 100
ELKINGTON, George Richards 32,
33, 45, 48, 51, 81, 107
ELKINGTON, J.B. 100
ELKINGTON, Mason & Co. 34, 45,
46, 50
ELKINGTONS 45
  Sons 52
ELLIOTT'S Metal Company Ltd 54
ERDINGTON 56, 98
  Bell Lane 65, 69, 79
  Birches Green 55
  Gravelly Hill 98
  Holly Lane 55
  Methodist Chapel 15, 16
  Orphanage 56
  Orphanage Road 65, 69
  Parish Registers 123
  Sheep Street 17, 56, 69
  Station Road 16, 56, 57, 69
  Vicar 123
ERDINGTON Historical Society 115
ESSEX 103
EUROPE 49
EXHIBITION 46
  Great 1851 46, 49

FACTORIES 25, 28
  Hours 39
  Inspector 37
  Inspector's Report 37
  Nickel Refining 55
FAMILY Tree Appendix 1
FECKENHAM 65
FINANCIAL Times 69
  Editor 69
FIRTH 85
FLUFF and Rough 81
FOWLER, Mr 19
FOWLER, L.W. 23
FRIENDS, Society of 68

GAUDET, Dr. 23
GERMANY 48
GILLOTT, Joseph 27, 29 117
GLASSWORKS 10, 120
GRAND Tour 24, 120
GREAT Levy Book 107
GRIFFIN'S Hill 107
GRIFFITHS, Elizabeth 1
GRIFFITHS, Richard 3, 10, 14, 15, 57
GRIFFITHS, Miss 79
GULLY, Dr. 23
GUN Making 25

HAHEMANN, Samuel 68
HARRIS, Arthur 21
HARRISON, Samuel 12, 15
HEATON, Ralph 113
HEELEY, James 12, 15
HELMINSTER, Miss 79
HESLOP, Thomas Pretious, Dr. 43,
86, 106
HINGLEY, John 84
HODGKISS, W. 87
HOLLAND, Henry 65
HOLLIDAY, F 81
HOLYOAKE, George Jacob 17,
69, 74, 111
HOMEOPATHIC Hospital 102
HOMEOPATHY 68, 81
HORSFALL, Thomas Coghlan 98
HORTON, Isaac 56, 81, 83, 86, 100
HUXLEY, Thomas Henry 91

ILFORD 103
ILLNESS 23, 118
INDIA Rubber Ring 50
  Experiments 48
  Cold converting process 51
INDUSTRIALISTS 5
INK Stands 27
IRELAND, George 52
IRONMONGER 35, 50, 55, 100
ITALIAN, Military Officer 118

JAMES, Paul Moon 99
JEFFERIES, Mrs 77
JEVONS, Solomon 68, 80, 81
JEWELLERY 10, 48
JOHN Bull 69
JOHNSON, G.J. 15, 25, 43, 63, 65,
81, 86, 87, 88, 92, 103, 105

KIDDERMINSTER 10, 57, 91
  Parish Church 1
  Richard Baxter's Chapel 9
  Summer Place Land Society 103
KING Edwards Schools 96
KNIGHTHOOD 110
KRUPP 48, 49

LANCASTER Street, 12, 13, 28, 33,
34, 40, 42, 43, 52, 71, 120
LAND 66, 103
LARKIN, Mr 77
LAURENCE Street Chapel 17
LEA, G. Rev. 19, 58, 60
LEADER, R.E. 45, 48
LEGGE Street 10
LIBERAL 4
LIBRARIES, Free 104, 106
LIVERPOOL 22, 49
LODGE, Oliver, Sir. 114
LONDON 45, 49
  University 91
LOUIS, Dr. 23

MACINTOSH 50, 51
MALVERN 23
MANCHESTER 44, 51, 72, 85, 98, 99
MANDER, Charles 98
MASON, Annie 16, 24, 51,
56, 119, 120
MASON, Elizabeth 1, 3
MASON, Hannah 1
MASON, Josiah, Sir.
  Achievements 1
  Art 89, 109
  Attempt to adopt 21
  Beggars 21
  Berwood House 107
  Birth place 1, 6
  Birthday 75, 89
  Burial 123
  Business 21, 24
  Chairman, B'ham Banking Co. 100
  Copper smelting 53
  Correspondence 19
  Cremation 124
  Death 122
  Death Certificate 122
  Description 72, 81, 83, 112
  Dinner Party 121
  Dogs 81

144

Donations   102
Education   3, 10
Electro-plating   26, 32, 34, 45, 49
Endowment   17
Erdington Turnpike Trust   102
Father   1, 3, 6, 8
Forks & Spoons   48, 50
Formation of new company   40
Funeral   122
Gardening   118
"Grand Tour"   24
Grandfather   3
Great Nephew   21, 122
Health concerns   23
Homeopathic Hospital   102
House in Harborne Road   107
Illness   23, 118, 121
Inventions   33, 34
Investment   103
Knighthood   89, 110
Land holdings   103
Land, schedule to Railway Act   98
Last illness   121
Laurence Street Chapel   17
Letter to H. Penn   113
Letter to Mayor   63
Letter to Rev. J.C. Miller   58
Letter to Thos Avery   87
Marriage   3, 25
Mother   3, 8, 9
Mourning Card   123
Nephew, Isaac Smith   34
Nickel refining   54
Norwood House   60
Offers for Company   40
Orphanage   16, 60
Partnership   49
Philanthropy   4, 5, 13, 17, 21,
                              56, 111, 117
Photograph   113
Phrenology   23
Politics   4, 21
Portrait   110, 111, 112
Power and influence   21, 103
Poverty   6, 21
Property   87
Purchase Price   41
Railway Company   98
Religion   4
Religious Views   19
Self-made Man   6
Selling door-to-door   8

Senile Decay   122
Servants   77
Slade House   107
Solicitor   103
Split ring works   12, 15, 33
Statue   113, 115
Train Accident   24
Trustees   60
Uncle   3, 10
Unemployment   12
Views on Clergy   20
Wealth   21, 103
Work   10, 12
Wife   16, 24, 107, 119, 120
Will   103, 124
MASON, Richard   1, 33
MASON, William   1, 10
MASON House   69
MASON, Hayes & Co.   55
MASON'S College (see Science College)
MASON'S Court   70
MASON'S University College
      Court of Governors   96
      Act   96
MATTHEWS, J.R.   72, 74
MAUSOLEUM   121
      Inscription on windows   121
      Vault   121
MENDELSOHN   91
MERMAID   71, 95
METHODIST, Newtown Row
                      Circuit   16
MIDDLEMORE, Mr   19
MIDLAND Institute (see B.M.I.)
MILL, J.S.   85
MILL Street   6, 10, 14
MILLER, Rev. J.C.   17, 19, 57
      Letter to   18
MITCHELL, John   27
MORTMAIN, Statute   63, 87
MUFFLES   33
MUNNS, Henry Turner   112
MUNTZ, Philip Henry   86, 105

NADEN, Constance   96
NATURE   13
NETTLEFOLD & Chamberlain   92
NETTLEFOLD & Co.   34
NETTLEFOLD, Joseph Henry   40
NEWHALL Street   45, 46, 50
NEWMAN, Cardinal   85
NEWTOWN Row, Circuit   16

145

NEWEY, Isaac 56
NICHOLSON, Miss 72
NICKEL
   Plating 54
   Refining 54
NICKEL Co. Ltd.
   Erdington 55
   London 55
NON-CONFORMIST 5, 14, 54
   Business Community 14
   Worship 14
NON-SECTARIAN 19, 63
   Education 19
NORTH, Isaac 68
NORTHFIELD 65
NORWOOD House 60, 65, 77,
   79, 103, 107, 112, 118, 121
   Picture Gallery 89
   Description 109

OLDBURY 29
OLTON 69
ORPHANAGE 16, 19, 43, 56
   Admission to Science College 88
   Badge 96
   Boys 65
   Boys house 72
   Bricks 61
   Chapel 68
   Children 58, 65
   Demolished, first 57
   Demolition 69
   Description 60
   Dining Room 68, 72
   Endowment 63, 103
   First, description 56
   Foundation Stone 60
   Girls 56, 57, 65
   Health Care 68, 81
   Inverness Capes 72
   Land 98
   Letter to Mayor 63
   Meeting of Religious Groups 58
   Mermaid 71
   Motto 71
   New wing 68
   Opening Ceremony 60
   Qualifications for Admission 65
   Railway line 98
   Religious needs 68
   Reunions 69
   Sale of land 69, 70

School 69
School subjects 66
Site 60
Staff 66
Towers 60
Trustees 60, 63, 65, 68, 105
Trust Deed 63, 65
Visiting 66
ORPHANS 13
   Accidents 76
   Admissions 65, 68, 71, 72
   Animals 79
   Apprenticeships 83
   Breakfast 76
   Cattle Show Outing 75
   Changes 84
   Chores 77, 78
   Clothes 71
   Christmas 75, 80
   Dentist 81
   Description of Mason 81, 83
   Food 76, 78, 79, 80
   Formal Entertainment 79
   Gardening 79
   Guy Fawkes 76
   Kitchen 77
   Laundry 77
   Leaving arrangements 83
   Matron 71
   Mason's Birthday 75
   May Day 76
   Medical attention 81
   Norwood House visits 77
   "Pancake Day" strike 74
   Play 79
   Pranks 78
   Punishments 73, 74
   Recreation Room 79
   Religious Services 79
   Smallpox 71
   Sport 76
   Sutton Park Outing 75
   Typical Day 76
   Visitors 76
   Weak eyes 72
OWEN, Robert 17
OWENS 85
OXFORD University 91

PALMER 25, 63, 106
PAPER Clips 27
PARIS 23, 24

146

PARKES, Alexander   45, 46, 50,
                    52, 55, 56
PARKES, Howard C.   40
PARSONS   79
PEART   27
PEMBREY   53
PENS   10
    Manufacture   29, 33, 34
    Persian   32
    Production figures   27, 28, 29, 34
    Quill   27
    Steel   12, 26, 27, 35
    Steel B   32
    Types   34
    Works   33
PENN, H.   113
PENNS   16
PENNS Lane   16
PENNEY, Christine   96
PERRY & Co.   26, 28, 43
PERRY & Co. Ltd.   34, 40, 42
PERRY Barr   124
PERRY, Edmund Stephen   43
PERRY, J.J.   40, 42, 43
PERRY, James   27, 40, 43
PERRY, L.H.   40
PEYTON'S   34
PHILANTHROPY   13, 17, 56
POLLACK, M.   34, 42, 105
POOLE, Philip   34
POYNTING, J.H. Dr.   96
PRINCE ALBERT   46
PRINCESS Alice Orphanage   68
PRINCIP Street   87
PROFESSORS   121
PROTESTANTS   19, 64
PUXTY, Mr.   73, 85

QUEEN VICTORIA   96, 110
QUEEN'S College   86, 88
    Clergy   85
    Medical Faculty   96
QUEEN'S Hospital   106
QUILLS   27

RAILWAY Line
    Eastern   98
    Western   98
READ, Mrs   79
READ, J.T.   74
RELIGIOUS Services   79
RENOLDS   44

ROMAN CATHOLIC   19
ROSE, Hyla, H. Rev.   123
ROSLYN, Guy   113
RUGBY   72
RUTHIN   51

SALFORD   34
SALTLEY   98
SAMSUN, Stephen   33
SCIENCE College   13, 19, 34
    Appointment of Professors   88
    Boardroom   113
    Builder   87
    Completed   91
    "Conversazione"   92
    Costs   93
    Court of Governors   96
    Curriculum   88
    Demolition   97
    Description   92
    Endowments   93, 96
    Famous Students   96
    Foundation Deed   87
    Foundation Stone   13
    Mason's University College   96
    Mermaid & Motto   95
    Opened   91
    Opening Ceremony   91
    Play of Professors & Assistants   88
    Plans   87
    Plaque   97
    Statue   113
    Subjects   88
    Teacher Training   96
    Trustees   86, 92, 105
SELF-HELP   13
SELLY Oak Colleges   107
SHAW, George   43, 86, 88, 99
SHAW, Thomas   68
SHEFFIELD   45, 85
    Steel   29
SHOP   9
SHOWROOMS   49
SIEMEN, G.W. Dr.   33
SIEMEN, Otto   33
"SIR JOSIAH MASON'S CO. LTD.   42
SIR JOSIAH MASON TRUST   70
SKIPP, V.   117
SLADE House   107
SLITTING   29
SMILES, Samuel   13
SMITH, Isaac   33, 34

147

SMITH, John O.M. 44
SMITH, Martyn Josiah 21, 32, 55, 122
SMITH, William 33
SOMERSET 71
SOMERVILLE & Co. 32, 33, 34, 40, 42, 43
SOLICITOR 15, 25, 43, 63, 106
SPENCER, Herbert 85
SPLIT Rings 12, 15, 33
ST. AGNES Convent 110

ST. EDMUNDS Campion 110
ST. MARTIN'S 17, 19, 57
STOCKWIN, Ann 66, 80
STOCKWIN, Caroline 66, 71, 72, 80
SUCKPLING, Mr 76
SUNDAY School 3, 9, 10, 16, 21, 52
SUTTON Coldfield 65

TANNER, Joseph 32
TARMAC Ltd 115
TAYLOR, Lucy 1, 97
THOMAS, Wynne, Dr. 68, 79
THOMASON, Edward, Sir. 45
TOWN Council 63, 68, 105
TOWYN Bach 53
TRUST DEED
   of Foundation of Orphanage 63, 65
TRUSTEES (see orphanage or Science
                                        college)
TUBB, A 123
TURNER, Mr 73
TURNPIKE Trust 102
TYBURN 76
TYNDALL, Johnson & Tyndall 40, 63

UNITARIAN 3, 9, 14, 17, 19, 21, 96

VICTORIA Federal University 88
VICTORIAN 97, 117

WALMLEY 76
WALSALL 52
WARDEN, W.M. 100
WARWICKSHIRE 65
   Lord Lieutenant 110
WEAVERS 3
   Bombazine 3
WEBSTER, Joseph 16
WEDLEY, L.L. 1
WESLEYAN 12, 17, 21
   Chapel 14
   Newtown Row Circuit 16
WEST Midlands 103
WHEELWRIGHT, William 16
WHITE, J.E. 37
WILL
   Mason's 103, 124
WILLIAMSON, F.G. 113
WINWOOD, Hannah, Miss 77, 79, 110
WILEY & Co. 43
WILEY, W.E. 40, 42, 43
WILSON, Dr. 24
WOODBROOKE 45, 107
WOLVERHAMPTON 98
WOMEN 51, 56
WORCESTERSHIRE 65
WORKERS
   Apprenticeships 51
   Agreements 51
   Boys 32
   "Carders" 32
   Children 37
   Girls 32
   "Foggers" 32
   Men 35
   Prizes 51
   Women 32
WORKSHOPS 25
WRIGHT, Benjamin, Rev. 79
WRIGHT, John 45

YEOMANS, John Christopher 68, 81
YENTON Primary School 69
YOUTH 13